CHOICE, CONTRACT, CONSENT:
A RESTATEMENT OF LIBERALISM

CHOICE, CONTRACT, CONSENT: A RESTATEMENT OF LIBERALISM

Anthony de Jasay

IEA

Institute of Economic Affairs
1991

First published in June 1991
by
THE INSTITUTE OF ECONOMIC AFFAIRS
2 Lord North Street, Westminster, London SW1P 3LB

Hobart Paperback 30

ISSN 0309-1783
ISBN 0-255 36246-3

*The Institute gratefully acknowledges financial support for its publications
programme and other work from a generous benefaction by the late Alec
and Beryl Warren.*

Printed in Great Britain by
Goron Pro-Print Co. Ltd., Lancing, W. Sussex

Filmset in 'Berthold' Times Roman 11 on 12 point

CONTENTS

FOREWORD

Graham Mather
General Director,
Institute of Economic Affairs

THE INTERACTION between philosophy and economics is one of the deepest and most stimulating fields for study. For economists, their work is enriched when the signals, choices and structures on which the economic market operates are considered in the broader context of human freedoms. Philosophical issues can be clarified when subjected to the framework and discipline of economic markets.

The task, however, requires formidable skills. For even the most acute and sharp-eyed analyst the language of rights in philosophy presents a myriad of confusions and difficulties. The origin and definition of rights, their relationship to considerations of sovereignty, welfare, equality, fairness, and justice, all present constant temptations towards subjectivity and confusion. This difficulty is easily passed across into economics. Applied macro-economics in particular tends to seek some form of grounding in philosophical doctrine, involving difficult questions on distribution and on the border between market and state.

Do these problems matter? Are they, in any event, capable of resolution or clarification? Are there philosopher-economists currently at work whose skills are sufficiently developed to disentangle the confusions of philosophers and raise the sights of economists?

It seems to me that the problems are important. Confusion of language is of especial concern in the area of rights, which tend to form the root of much philosophical, political and economic discourse. The distinctive mission of the Institute of Economic

Affairs is to educate the public through scholarly research and publication in precisely such areas, enjoined as it is in its statutes to study the 'effect of moral and political factors on the operation of economic laws'. And as the work of, among others, Mr Samuel Brittan of the *Financial Times* and Dr John Gray of Oxford has shown,[1] fruitful advance can be secured by imaginative scholarship in this terrain.

Anthony de Jasay brings formidable skills to the task. A former lecturer in economics at Oxford, he is a philosopher of international distinction. Jasay's *The State*[2] is a powerful treatment of the state's rôle; recently, in *Social Contract, Free Ride*,[3] he developed his study of the interplay between economic and societal questions.

In *Choice, Contract, Consent* Anthony de Jasay proceeds, as ever, from fundamentals. He begins with the essence of liberalism. He examines with scrupulous care the confusion and 'doctrinal decomposition' which in his view require a stricter redefinition of liberalism. He proceeds to establish this, but in doing so is careful to distinguish between procedural and ultimate 'metaphysical' commitments—amongst other things, people's sense of what is proper and fitting, and people's preparedness to award themselves rights.

Leaving open these choices is important: for some, in the tradition of Professor Sir Ralf Dahrendorf's recent work, would consider that the preparedness of societies to institutionalise entitlements presents an alternative model. This institutional rather than individual liberalism would, they consider, reflect an alternative approach although the practical result may turn out to be not dissimilar to that envisaged by the present author.

Such an approach reminds the reader of the most important contribution of the public choice school headed by the Nobel laureate, Professor James Buchanan. Public choice liberals in this tradition may also look to some institutionalisation—for example in collective financing of education, or collective redress of major

---

[1] Samuel Brittan, *A Restatement of Economic Liberalism*, London: The Macmillan Press, 1988; John Gray, *Limited Government: A Positive Agenda*, Hobart Paper No. 113, London: Institute of Economic Affairs, 1989.

[2] Oxford: Blackwells, 1985.

[3] Oxford: The Clarendon Press, 1989.

intergenerational transfer of wealth—while regretting that governmental activity as it is today may not achieve desired goals through these means.

Addressing these issues imports subjective considerations, and sharp differences of view. Dr Gray's earlier IEA study put down some markers, and the debate will no doubt continue. Anthony de Jasay's contribution, however, is further removed. By seeking to redefine liberalism more strictly he makes the subsequent debates easier, and the relationships between philosophy and economics clearer. That is why, although the study represents the views and analysis of the author and not of the Institute, which never expresses a corporate view, its Directors, Managing Trustees or Advisers, it is offered as an important and helpful contribution to academic and public understanding and discussion.

June 1991   GRAHAM MATHER

THE AUTHOR

ANTHONY de JASAY has studied in Budapest, Perth
(Western Australia), and Oxford. He left his native Hungary
upon the change-over to the socialist régime in 1948. He was a
Research Fellow in Economics at Nuffield College, Oxford, from
1957-62. He then went into the finance and investment banking
business in Paris, 1962-79. For the last ten years he has made his
home in Normandy.

His scholarly interests have switched from economics to
political philosophy, which has resulted in two books: *The State*
(Oxford: Basil Blackwell, 1985); *Social Contract, Free Ride*
(Oxford: Clarendon Press, 1989). The Institute has previously
published his *Market Socialism: A Scrutiny* (Occasional Paper
No. 84, 1990).

INTRODUCTION

IT HAS become hard to decide who is *not* a liberal, and what liberalism is *not*. Looking back to the Scottish Enlightenment of Ferguson, Hume and Smith, to the sources of Continental liberalism in Wilhelm von Humboldt, Constant and Guizot, to the Whigs, to Tocqueville and Bastiat, over differences of focus one discerns a fair degree of ideological compatibility. There are reasonably homogeneous aims centred around the autonomy of the individual, to be left sovereign in choosing what he wants and free to contract with others for mutual gain. Put plainly, this liberalism is above all about 'freedom', and knows no other freedom than that of the individual.

As it evolves, the doctrine splits and splits again. At the turn of the century, *laissez-faire* ceases to be the guiding rule, to be respected except when it is very inconvenient not to cheat a little. In its place, liberalism consciously starts adopting multiple, opinion-bound and shifting criteria drawn from both general welfare, distributive considerations such as equality or 'fairness', and individual rights. In the last half-century, notably in legal thought and economics, liberalism gradually loses its discipline and its definite identity. Under the liberal label there is a barely compatible mixture of ends, leading to deep confusion, which no other major political ideology, not even socialism, has suffered to anything like the same extent.

Depending on who speaks, a 'liberal' policy today can mean one thing or its opposite. Unstable and uncertain language among classical, American and neo-liberals about freedom and 'rights', pulling policy in all directions at once, reflects the conceptual disarray.

Some would argue that this is a healthy evolution of a living theory, making room for a wide diversity of views, articulating the multiple interests and preferences of modern society. If it is a victory of applied, *ad hoc* reason over ideology, and of pragmatism over principle, so be it.

However, the victory of pragmatism over principle is nothing to be proud of. Others would admit this, yet plead that at the end of the day it is impossible to deduce a coherent set of liberal (or for that matter any other) principles from undisputed truths and generally shared goals in such a way that the resulting political theory should, in its essentials, resist the wear and tear of time and circumstance. In this view, as we build the Tower of Babel, principles will mutate, and our theory will divide over and over again—liberalism is particularly Protean in this respect—with liberals ending up speaking in many tongues. The founding fathers might take this for incoherent babble, but they would be mistaken. It is simply what happens as liberalism lives up to some of its own liberal precepts.

Taking this view is to condemn liberalism to a progressive loss of identity.

The present paper reflects a triple belief. *First*, a coherent and stable political theory is good for ordering society's relations with its government. It does not guarantee good or at least limited government—probably nothing does—but it helps to define the sort of limits we should do well to aim at. *Second*, setting such a theory in the concrete of undisputed first principles is a difficult but attractive enough enterprise to be tried even if success is not assured. *Third*, the intellectual decomposition of liberalism was not due to the march of history, but to the softness of its building blocks and to a design that positively invited tinkering, adding to, reforming.

Part One explores the causes of this decomposition and takes issue with some of the doctrines that remain within what I will refer to as Loose Liberalism. Part Two is an attempt at a simplified design for Strict Liberalism, derived from first principles. I think it is best assessed in juxtaposition with its loose counterpart.

Part One
LOOSE LIBERALISM

1

THE CONFUSION
OF TONGUES

1. Pluralism

It IS frequently suggested that the apparent indeterminacies of liberalism are due to its very virtue: for it is liberal in the literal meaning of the word. It admits that there are many 'values' (non-instrumental ends) worth pursuing, and no reason to suppose that all, or indeed more than a small handful at a time, can be fitted without conflict and friction into a political and social order.[1] Harsher ideologies—nationalism, socialism or dull old conservatism—seek to subjugate the conflict by rejecting, suppressing or studiously ignoring values that clash with their principal ends. Liberalism, on the contrary, is pluralistic. It is essentially tolerant of a multitude of ends, 'conceptions of the good', without asking that they be mutually compatible. Give and take is required to accommodate them, and trade-offs between values must be accepted as legitimate. Far from being a sign of conceptual confusion and the self-contradiction of a doctrine, liberal pluralism is actually a matter of consistency with the basic liberal principle, common to all its versions, of 'value-neutrality'.

This view is plausible. But is it right? Value-neutrality has at least two meanings. Taking one or the other has vastly different implications.

---

[1] *Cf.* Sir Isaiah Berlin, *Concepts and Categories*, London: The Hogarth Press, 1978, pp. xvi-xvii and p. 95.

5

Choice, Contract, Consent: A Restatement of Liberalism

(a) 'Pushpin and Poetry'

The first meaning is what, with Bentham, we might call the 'pushpin and poetry' view. Bentham, of course, meant that the same 'utility'-sum yielded by the one was no worse than that provided by the other, and that we must not be concerned with the moral worth of different sources of utility. But value-neutrality is by no means dependent on, nor is it confined to, a utilitarian framework. It is merely non-perfectionist, in that it leaves moral perfection—whether gleefully or regretfully, we need not ask—to its fate among the voluntary decisions of individuals in society.

This implies that it is not the business nor the right of the political authority to favour one value, say, poetry, over another, playing pushpin, even if the great and the good, the makers of public opinion and even the bulk of the electorate hold (as they presumably do) poetry to be the worthier of the two. For in that case they can form reading circles, buy books of verse, encourage poets, but ought not to expect the government to do it in their stead. A major principle stands in the way of that. Government is for better or worse endowed with exceptional, monopolistic coercive power. Even its powers in persuasion and education are ultimately dependent on its power to tax. Such awesome power must be subject to definite limitations based on stable principles, one of which is precisely value-neutrality in the pushpin-and-poetry sense.

The consent that legitimises state coercion can be sweepingly construed as a general mandate to carry out 'society's will', whatever that may be. If society expresses its wishes by majority voting (which is what we are expected to believe in this democratic age), the government's warrant simply reads: 'You are to do what you must to earn majority support'. Should the majority seem to think that poetry ought to get state help, it is not only legitimate but mandatory to spend tax money on poets and their verse. However, no normative political doctrine would put such an openly cynical construction on the consent to be taxed as 'consent for the money to be spent to keep the government in power'. That consent has this practical effect is arguable, but few would hold that it is desirable, if only because of the disturbing implication that no principle is left standing to impose self-restraint on a government fully obedient to electoral expediency.

Value-neutrality, at all events, is inspired by very different, essentially moral considerations—paradoxical as it may sound to ascribe a neutral stand on moral values, of all things, to morality.

The strongest reason why a principle admits that people as individuals, or acting through voluntary associations, should promote a value, but refuses to admit that they may legitimately instruct their supposed agent, the government, to do it for them, is complex, but once clearly stated, its basic element is quite simple. Such terms as 'society', 'nation' or 'community' insidiously suggest some entity that can will an end, and must will the corresponding means as a matter of non-self-contradiction. 'It' values and demands poetry; consistency and honesty require that 'it' should concede tax expenditures on poetry's behalf commensurate with the value 'it' puts on poetry.

However, if there *were* such an entity, and it had a single mind, a will and a purse, it would not need the coercive agency of government to find the means and apply them to the end it willed. It would choose the end and fit the means to it, in a single act, all by itself. It is only because there is no such entity, but only aggregations of individuals having their own wills, that there is any rôle at all for a government, able to coerce some persons to contribute means to a particular end they may be at best lukewarm about, but which other people value highly.

(In practice, especially if the means involved are a mere drop in the ocean of public expenditure, those who press for the state to foster a particular value usually do not consciously realise that they are by the same token demanding that others be made to pay for it—others who *ex hypothesi* do not sufficiently care for it to pay without being forced to do so.)

That a liberal government is value-neutral means neither that it *is* insensitive and indifferent between, say, junk and great art, nor does it mean that it is *not*. It simply means that it is not morally empowered to give practical effect to its *own* predilections if it could indulge them only by imposing costs on its subjects.

This, then, is the practical effect of the pushpin-and-poetry version of value-neutrality. Its principle is altogether consistent with the original image of liberalism as a doctrine of personal autonomy and severely limited government. In fact, this doctrine *presupposes* the principle, for a value-fostering government could

7

not remain limited even if it tried, and would betray its vocation by trying.

We do know, however, that many purported liberals now reject the doctrine of limited government, insisting that if limits are set, they should not be such as to hamper the government in doing good.

(b) Let a Hundred Flowers Bloom

Strangely, such a position is *also* supported by value-neutrality, albeit in another of its versions. This 'hundred-flowers' version arises from the view that one violates neutrality by omission no less than by commission. Some flowers bloom unaided, others need tending. Some thrive, others wither in the competitive, mercenary climate of a market economy. (The blooming and withering rôles would, of course, be reversed in a Spartan military state, or in an Egyptian or Aztec theocracy.) Standing by passively for the sake of limiting the scope of government is really to favour one type of flower, one value over another.

Such a bias is arbitrary, both because the ends that tend to wither as a result are morally no less valuable for that, and are quite likely to be more so, and because the people who attach very great value to the neglected ends are no less entitled to see them realised than those who are better served by the 'blind caprice of the market'. It behoves the impartial, value-neutral state to bring about equal opportunities with respect to both; every *value* must be enabled, by positive discrimination if need be, to flourish as richly as every other, and every *person* must have as much chance successfully to pursue his favourite ends as every other, regardless of which ones he pursues (as long as they are values and not wrongful ends). No artefact claiming to be art must be denied its share of public money on grounds that it is ugly, repulsive or boring; no one must be branded a drop-out, a 'weirdo', a pervert, and suffer deprivation by virtue of the 'counter-cultural' unorthodoxy of what he tries to express or the life he chooses to lead.

Admittedly, a closer inspection of 'hundred-flowers' neutrality shows it to be setting difficult, counter-intuitive requirements. By stipulating 'equal' favour to 'every' value, it seems to forbid priorities. Since the number of legitimate 'values' is indefinitely large, fostering each equally, or even to an equal degree of flourishing (whatever that would mean), would absorb indefinitely large resources unless the support for each was negligibly small. Nevertheless, 'hundred-flowers' is at first blush a possible interpretation of pluralist value-neutrality.

It has, moreover, an almost irresistible attraction. 'Pushpin and poetry' calls for fairly severe self-denial on the part of the government and those who, through their influence on opinion, help set its agenda. 'Let a hundred flowers bloom', on the other hand, encourages political activism, invites the largest possible number of pressure groups to come forward and demand support, and creates a climate in which government can flourish along with the values it fosters. Whether this is to be welcomed or deplored, it is fully consistent with what has become part of mainstream liberal thought.

Thus we find two versions of value-neutrality to imply two antagonistic principles, and to entail diametrically opposed guidance to policy. The historically prior 'pushpin' version requires that *to each, his value. Let him realise it as best he can.* Coercion must not be imposed on others to make them help him. The more recent 'hundred-flowers' version prescribes *to each value, equal chances.* By the default of civil society, it is left to the state to make them equal.

If there is really room within liberalism for both doctrines, it is pluralist indeed. But then it can hardly continue to claim to have a recognisable identity.

2. The Goal and the Rule

With hindsight, the identity troubles of liberalism could probably have been predicted from the underlying logical *structure* of its theory, which is largely responsible for its *contents* having been turned into variable matters of opinion. Like many other political theories, the structure of liberalism is constructed of two elements:

(i) A maximisation postulate: political arrangements are judged according to their expected contribution to an overriding goal. Their purpose is its fulfilment to the greatest feasible extent. If, for example, the maximand is national power, the corresponding theory would recommend political arrangements best suited to promoting defence, investment and population growth, and to discouraging self-indulgence by the citizenry.

(ii) Observance of a rule (or rule-system). Whatever else political arrangements are designed to do, they must do it within this rule. One characteristic rule is simply conformity of policy to the country's constitution (whose substantive content may be outlined by a subsidiary theory); or that natural justice should prevail; or that certain equalities among persons should be enforced.

Generally, a political theory can be interpreted as having a foot in both (i) and (ii). Its typical design is to promote the *maximand*, and also to observe the *rule*. However, the two are usually in conflict at their respective margins: the stricter is obedience to the rule, the more maximisation of the objective is constrained, and *vice-versa*. (Modern rule-utilitarianism, however, provides a subtle example of the opposite relation or at least the expectation of it: the rule is to observe a particular set of moral precepts, and obedience to this rule is meant to be actually conducive to maximum utility over a long enough period.)

Ostensibly, priority of passage can be given to the *maximand*, or to the rule. If the *maximand* is accorded priority, the theory in fact calls for 'constrained maximisation' within the space left by the rule. By way of example: (maximisation) we aim at the fastest economic growth we can achieve, (+ rule) compatible with preserving the quality of the environment. Precisely the same type of prescription results if we reverse the apparent priority: (rule) human rights must not be violated, (+ maximisation) the public interest must prevail subject to non-violation of human rights.[1] Asking which has the priority, or which is really subject to which, is as senseless as Alfred Marshall's leading question about which blade of the scissors cuts the cloth.

Assigning the priority rôle to the goal or to the rule, though illusory, has nevertheless some symbolic significance. It helps

---

[1] By its nature, a rule is absolute and cannot have exceptions. However, a well-founded political theory, while not formally admitting exceptions, will so formulate its rules that they should not, or not mandatorily, cover cases the theory may wish to exempt for reasons of convenience or 'overall benefit'. (*Cf.* A. Gewirth, 'Are There Any Absolute Rights?', in J. Waldron (ed.), *Theories of Rights*, New York: OUP, 1984, p. 95.)

to set the tone of a political theory, and conditions its choice of language. Thus, two liberal theories can have the same structure, yet one will declare itself freedom-oriented (maximising it), the other 'rights-based' (setting the rule that a particular list of rights must be respected and enforced). The alleged priority of freedom in the first theory, and of rights in the second, will hardly have practical consequences, except in the manner in which each will justify largely identical precepts.

The relation of a political theory to a political community is either to diagnose, or to set norms. In diagnosis, it is used to understand existing political arrangements. What *maximand*, if any, are they designed to serve?—what rule are they supposed to observe? The normative use of the theory, on the other hand, is to deduce the arrangements that would best promote the chosen goal while conforming to the chosen rule. Liberalism, no less than other political theories, should lend itself to these standard approaches. Yet it is as capable of commending a particular political practice or institution as it is of condemning it. The culprit for this slipperiness is the woolly content given to its maximisation-and-rule-obedience framework. Very broadly speaking, its maximand is freedom, and its rule is that the exercise of freedom can be constrained to protect the interests of others.

With some exceptions, liberal theorists use a fairly general, albeit usually vague, concept of freedom, not confined to the 'political freedoms' of speech, assembly and election, intended to enable individuals to influence collective choices. However, the notion of freedom is notoriously malleable. There is almost boundless latitude to the meanings that can be read into it. The interests whose protection is a legitimate ground for limiting freedom are likewise open to a wide range of, in part mutually contradictory, interpretations. With regard to both freedom and the interests across which it must not trespass, one can only take positions that are ultimately subjective, 'unprovable', supported by intrinsically unwinnable, contestable but unrebuttable arguments. Within loose limits, disparate contents can be read into freedom and nearly any interest can be claimed to be sufficient ground for an inviolable right.

It is this latitude that is arguably the root cause of liberalism's progressive loss of firm contours and rigorous content.

2

FREEDOM

1. 'Having One's Way'

AT THE risk of labouring the obvious, we may remind ourselves why freedom must not stand by itself as a goal, and must be held in by a suitable set of rules. In fact, the nature of these rules is one of the most contentious aspects of political theory.

We read of the Russian peasant, a man surely unspoilt by too much freedom, that

'[H]is fondest wish was to be totally, irresponsibly free. His word for this ideal condition was *volia*, a word meaning "having one's way". To have *volia* meant to enjoy licence: to revel, to carouse, to set things on fire. . . . The literary critic Vissarion Belinskii . . . put the matter bluntly . . .:

"Our people understand freedom as *volia*, and *volia* for it means to make mischief. The liberated Russian nation would not head for the parliament but it would run for the tavern to drink liquor, smash glasses and hang the *dvoriane* who shave their beards and wear frock-coats . . ."[1]

Maximisation of freedom in the crude sense of all having their way, means in a first approximation that there are no obstacles erected by the authority responsible for freedom-maximising to what each may do, including the making of mischief. According

---

[1] R. Pipes, *Russia Under the Old Regime*, New York: Charles Scribner's Sons, 1974, pp. 156-57.

to a widely accepted, though dubious, twofold classification, this would mean that everybody's 'negative' freedom was as great as possible. Maximising 'positive' freedom, in turn, would increase, up to the limit of their physical availability, all the scarce opportunities for making (non-trivial) choices, including mischief-making. More hayricks to burn would mean greater positive freedom.

Obviously, these meanings would be unacceptable. Nor does it help to refine them by a distributive sub-clause, stipulating equality. Philosophers of freedom, notably Kant and Herbert Spencer, used this stipulation to take care of the freedom of others that may be affected by the freedom of one. They required 'equal freedom' for all. The influential American liberal, John Rawls, also formulated his maximising principle with heavy, and unnecessary, emphasis on the equality of everyone's freedom:

> 'Each person is to have an *equal* right to the most extensive total system of *equal* basic liberties *compatible with a similar system of liberty for all.*'[1]

Simply barring the italicised words would leave the meaning wholly intact. Since everyone has a right to the same system, the rights are *ipso facto* equal rights to the system of liberties, and if everyone has the same one, they must by definition be compatible with all having them.

However, the redundant stress on equality does not in fact make the freedom-maximising principle any less problematical. For unless 'a system of liberties' is defined with great care,[2] its *equal* distribution among persons affords no protection against each being damaged by the other's freedom; if anything, the damage is liable to be more widespread than under an unequal distribution. For if *A* is free to burn hayricks, *B* must be 'equally' free to burn them, including those of *A*. Both enjoy the greatest possible 'negative' freedom from government interference and statutory obstacles. Their 'positive' freedom is maximised by open access to all existing hayricks. Unfortunately, the reciprocal damage to each other's interests takes away all satisfaction they might have found in their freedom being 'equal' to everybody else's.

[1] J. Rawls, *A Theory of Justice*, Oxford: OUP, 1972, p. 302 (my italics).
[2] *Ibid.*, p. 202.

Leaving aside the question whether one person's freedom can ever be said, except colloquially, to be 'equal' to another's—for it is far from clear that they possess enough common quantitative features to make them at all commensurate—the lesson one draws from *volia* is that the maximisation of freedom as unrestricted free choice can rapidly lead to absurd implications. It begs the question of the constraining rules that would save it from absurdity.

2. Coercion, and Arbitrary Will

Under the 'having one's way' principle, all depends on the constraining rule adopted to stop maximisation from running amok. There are, however, other, and less crude, current principles that make the freedom requiring to be constrained rather more tame.

Hayek has proposed two, both relating to what some would call 'negative' freedom.[1] One is that coercion should be at its 'necessary' minimum. This condition can be put to two possible uses.

(a) *'Non-coercion'* would be 'having one's way'. *Minimal* coercion would mean that freedom in some proper, non-absurd sense *has* been maximised. For this sense to be clear, the understanding of coercion must be clear.

An action or threat thereof, *intended to change* the value (cost) of *another's options for the worse* to an extent *sufficient to impose* the choice of some or *to bar* others and to provide *moral absolution* to the coercee for yielding to the threat, is *prima facie* wrongful, a tort.

However, any political theory that accepts the state reserves for it a category of coercion which is not wrongful but legitimate for some reason. Any liberal theory, loose or strict, is concerned with finding the limits beyond which coercion by the state ceases to be legitimate. For classical liberals and, less pronouncedly,

---

[1] F. A. Hayek, *The Constitution of Liberty*, London: Routledge & Kegan Paul; Chicago: University of Chicago Press, 1960, Ch. 1. The same work provides, in notes 14, 15, 21, 23 and 26 on pp. 423-25, a bibliography on 'positive' and 'negative' freedom with excerpts illustrating the boundless confusion that springs from resorting to these notions. Note, in particular, John Dewey's jumble of words, which Hayek understandably qualifies as 'appalling'.

neo-liberals the essential part of the political agenda of a liberal régime is to narrow and harden these limits and to hold the state to them. (For libertarians and anarchists, there is of course no legitimate coercion, however little it may be.) Wherever the limits may lie, minimising coercion until they are reached adds nothing to the principle of freedom-maximisation—in a way, it is synonymous with it—and fails to provide the constraining rule that would fully protect people from each other's free choices.

(b) *'Necessary Coercion'* comes closer, in that it refers to some particular level or pattern of coercion, which is neither zero nor merely 'minimal', as the proper, damage-minimising limit to be aimed at. Where it is situated is far from evident. For all we know, it may actually be higher than the existing level. For Hayek, it is the level or pattern of coercion required to enforce the general body of law that holds in place the protective framework which responsible individuals need to lead their lives according to their own lights. A system of general law is in turn inspired by moral principles. The system compatible with 'minimum necessary coercion' is the one inspired by those moral principles that have proved themselves by 'natural selection', that is, by the greater success of societies adopting them.

Interpretation (b) is closer to Hayek's intentions than (a). At first sight, it offers a maximisation principle with its own built-in necessary constraining rule. If this were in fact the case, we should have here a strict, well-defined, non-malleable liberal doctrine. However, the appearance of strictness and determinacy, notably the test of success of a system of law, conceals some irreducible vagueness.

It is, namely, always possible for persons of the same culture widely to disagree on what it is to be a responsible individual, how one leads one's own life, and what constitutes the protective framework one needs for doing so. On each of these counts, one might well call for extensive state provision of what Hayek has elsewhere, a touch naïvely, called 'highly desirable' public goods and services 'which involve no coercion except for the raising of the means by taxation'.[1] Here is a clear call, or what anyone

---

[1] F. A. Hayek, *New Studies in Philosophy, Economics and the History of Ideas*, London: Routledge & Kegan Paul, 1978, p. 144.

might be excused for taking as one, to re-create something like the 'Swedish model'[1] under the liberal banner. Horrified as Hayek would be by the imputation of such a proposal, his exposition is fully consistent with it, and must be classed as 'loosely liberal' for that reason.

Moreover, the success or failure of societies neither is nor need be correlated with the system of law they obey and still less with the moral principles such law should be guided by. Historical success is, perhaps more than any other, essentially a product of multiple causation, as Hayek, who rightly despises theories of history, would be the first to admit. If only because the statistical sample—the number of societies adopting a given system of law—is quite small, there can be no serious attempt at separating out the effect of the morality of law from a multitude of other potential causes. Perhaps worse still, there is no objective test to compel agreement about what system of law a society in fact uses. Broad descriptions like 'a system recognising *habeas corpus*, private property and judicial review of administrative action' appear to fit too many societies with very different legal and political systems, according very different rôles to 'freedom'.

Finally, there is no generally valid, agreed test of a society's success; many of those who consider Sweden successful find the United States unsuccessful, and *vice-versa*. (Few, however, accept Hayek's own proposed test, a society's physical capacity to feed an ever-growing population. The incapacity to do so may be a proof of Russia's failure, but would the capacity have proved her success?)

(c) *'Arbitrary Will'* and the immunity from it that should be maximised, is Hayek's alternative way of designating freedom as the goal. It has the same seeming attraction of completeness and firmness as 'necessary coercion'. However, if we are to be immune from arbitrary will, we may yet be subject to will that is non-arbitrary. The line between the two, if there is a clearly visible one, is drawn by the law. For Hayek, that does not mean

---

[1] The 'Swedish model' is the widely used shorthand term for the goal of an advanced welfare state governed along social democratic principles, where the greater part of national income is devoted to transfer payments, public goods and government services.

the positive law we find in statute and precedent (legal positivism, leaving room for unjust law, is anathema to him), but the law that ought to be, that is inspired by the right moral principles—that is, whose rightness has been proved by their success in cultural selection. Hence all that makes 'necessary coercion' loose, impressionistic and indeterminate also undermines the fixity of 'arbitrary will'.

3. Having Palatable Options

'Positive' freedom has its own versions of the freedom-maximising principle. They are, however, a little harder to recognise as such than the 'negative' ones. I am reformulating them so they will fit into the order of the present argument.

(a) *'Free Agency'* claims that, other things being equal, freedom depends on the way a person's important, non-trivial options are situated in relation to one another. Among mutually exclusive alternatives (marry John, live with Richard, stay with Mum, become a nun, wash dishes in a café), the difference between the best and the next-worse must not be excessively large; the next-worse must not be *very much* worse. If it is, there is no 'real' or 'really acceptable' alternative to the better of two options (or the best of the set of several). Therefore the person choosing it was not 'really' free to choose anything else.

On this lack of a palatable alternative is based the well-known argument about wage-slavery; the choice between accepting and refusing to be exploited by some capitalist is no real choice. Starving being no 'real' alternative, the wage-earner is not a free agent.

Other stock examples are widely used to illustrate the purported difference between 'formal' freedom (there is only one 'real' option, the others being 'unacceptable') and 'real' freedom or free agency, the proper goal in freedom maximisation.

Significantly, the argument tends to rely on adjectives, such as 'real' or 'acceptable', in classifying alternative options. Such adjectives of course inject the element of an observer's subjective judgement that suffices to make subsequent conclusions necessarily indeterminate, 'observer-dependent'. It becomes impossible to find conclusively that a state of affairs does, or does not, meet the necessary conditions of the state of freedom. No argument

17

has much prospect of being decisive if it relies in an essential way on the effect of such words as 'real', 'acceptable', 'substantial', 'worthwhile', and so forth. These words cannot be altogether banned from non-quantitative analysis, but they must not carry the main weight—as they are made to do in the 'free agency' argument.

Free agency as a matter of 'real', 'acceptable' alternatives is more than free agency *tout court*. It is important for the critical understanding of liberal doctrine to appreciate this point. It is now widely regarded as an error to suppose (as Leibniz, the 17th-century founding father of rationalist philosophy, taught us to do) that everything, including every choice one makes, must have had sufficient cause. 'Uncaused', gratuitous choices can certainly be imagined. On any possible view, if ever we are free agents, we must be it when we act gratuitously. Most choices, however, can plausibly be assumed to have had sufficient cause. Choice 'caused' by the chooser's dispositions or preferences is the base hypothesis in all rational-choice theory. The hypothesis is used with particular rigour in economics. Is choice caused by preference compatible with free agency? The idea of 'real' alternatives as its pre-condition appears to entail that if one option is very much preferred to all others (either because it is so good, or because all others are so awful), the chooser is not a free agent. His choice has a cause that is 'too strong' to leave him any freedom.

Even if he acts spinelessly and dishonourably, he is morally excused because acting honourably would have been 'too costly'. *Cost* is thus allowed to play the rôle that in the common-and-garden meaning of free agency can be played only by coercion—a quite different concept.

However, this is taking liberties with moral philosophy. Setting a price, however outrageous, is in itself not coercive. It becomes coercive *when it changes for the worse the options* the 'coercee' *would otherwise have had*, and does so to a degree *sufficient to force him to change the choice* he would otherwise have made,[1] by the same token morally absolving him from blame for it. Coercion, unless made legitimate by the existence of sufficient cause, is therefore *prima facie* a tort. Setting a harsh price may be heartless, but it is not a tort.

---

[1] *Cf.* above, page 14.

Free agency does not depend on whether a person's choice is driven by a *strong* or a *weak* cause or *no cause* at all. It depends on the agent's capacity to choose from whatever alternatives he faces. He must be a sane adult and not be under duress. In the standard example of 'your money or your life', the victim who hands over his wallet is not a free agent, not because losing his life is so very much *worse*, but because handing it over is imposed, and keeping it is barred, by coercion.[1] On this view, there is no room for 'positive' freedom and all options need not be equally 'acceptable'. Non-coercion takes care of the requirements of the freedom principle. If public policy is expected to make available particular constellations of alternatives, so that they are all 'acceptable' and the best is not 'too costly' to reject, it must be in the name of some other goal, principle or norm.

(b) *More and Better Options* is an alternative postulate of 'positive freedom'. Free agency targeted the *difference* between the best and the next-worse alternative. 'More and better' focuses on the absolute *levels* and *numbers* of the available options. A person who lacks any palatable ones is thus to be judged unfree, even if 'technically' he is under no coercion to take any one of his equally poor, stunted alternatives, but can choose whichever leaves him least miserable.

In its basic form, this version of positive freedom is easy to dismiss. In straightforward language, the person in this predicament is not *unfree*—he is *poor*. Improving, widening, enriching his alternatives is neither more nor less than making him richer. The 'more and better' positive freedom principle would require us instead to say 'making him free'.

This usage is a code replacing ordinary language. It impairs its

---

[1] Hobbes, who uses this example in *Leviathan*, considers that *if* there is no 'Civill Law' against the victim being so threatened, he is entering into a mutually advantageous exchange contract with the 'Theefe', by buying his life for his purse. The implication is that in the absence of law, he has no right *not* to be threatened, hence the 'Theefe' did not coerce him by violating a right he did not have. (*Cf.* T. Hobbes, *Leviathan*, 1651, ed. C. B. Macpherson, London: Penguin, 1985, p. 198.)

The position set out in the text above differs from that of Hobbes in that its concepts of free agency and coercion are prior to law and right, and are not dependent on the latter. Coercion is defined without reference to a person's rights it would violate.

honesty, opens a broad gate to ever sloppier arguments, and deprives political programmes of the transparency we badly need in order to judge them. It is no gain for clarity if the agenda of the welfare state is not called the fight against poverty, but the fight for freedom.

The underlying fault seems to be to try to squeeze a new goal, 'wellbeing' or perhaps 'equal wellbeing', in with the old one, 'freedom'. Transforming the latter into a composite of 'negative' and 'positive' freedom is a verbal sleight-of-hand.

However, the sleight-of-hand is not gratuitous; it has its uses. Some modern liberal theorists, like most illiberal ones, want the state (or as they persist in putting it, 'society') to help the options of the poor by taking resources away from the rich. Actions through either the revenue or the expenditure side of the state's budget, or through the direct 're-arrangement' of property rights, are designed to achieve this end. One kind of measure is not particularly favoured over the other. Where liberals differ from others is in their efforts to show that the coercion involved is employed to maximise *freedom*. The benign consequence for freedom ought to make coercion acceptable in the eyes of those who would question redistribution undertaken for some other avowed purpose.

These freedom-oriented arguments are directed at the distribution of wealth and the opportunities it alone creates (for opportunities that do not depend on material wealth, but can be created without prior resource transfers—for instance, by changing eligibility rules for career openings—are not grounds for redistributing wealth). They are more roundabout than the basic 'poverty is unfreedom' argument. Whether they carry more weight I will not attempt to judge here. My purpose is only to illustrate how they succeed in stretching the scope of liberal theory and how they dilute the characteristics of what we are supposed to accept as a liberal order, so that a wide range of mutually contradictory positions can be accommodated within it.

They do not directly identify the number and attractiveness of options with freedom, nor freedom with the political system's final, non-instrumental end. Instead, they employ intermediate stratagems. One is to claim, not that improving options is an increase of freedom, but that it enhances the 'worth of freedom'.[1]

---

[1] Rawls, *op. cit.* p. 204.

Another is to represent both the uncoerced access to options and their quantity and quality as instrumental to further, more nearly final ends.[1] Among such goals, we are offered: the realisation of individuals' 'life plans', their capacity to 'create their own lives', to 'pursue projects', to attain 'their conception of the good', and so forth. For these ends, free access to trivial options is irrelevant. The freedom 'to talk to Jones', 'to cut down trees in the next field', to pick 'a certain choice of ice-cream'[2] can safely be denied. Indeed, coercion may actually promote autonomy: 'some options one is better off not having'.[3]

Moreover, government may coerce people 'in order to force them to take actions . . . to improve people's options . . .'.[4] The coercion involved infringes some people's autonomy, but this is justified on the ground that it also increases that of the same people or of others.[5] The latter conclusion, approving the trade-off of some people's interest for that of others, is an explicit affirmation that interpersonal comparisons of interests are legitimate. A crucial rôle is thus reserved for subjective opinion, which is of course the sole possible arbiter of policies that favour some at the expense of others.

Interpersonal comparisons have been inseparable from earlier formulations of utilitarian liberalism, but have been mostly abandoned as dubious metaphysics. They are now filtering back into circulation, no longer as quantitative estimates of utilities, but as avowed moral judgements. There are frequent examples of them in current liberal literature. They can increase the 'pluralism' of the doctrine, the discretion it allows, its power to promote a variety of intrusive policies, by several orders of magnitude.

This power is compounded by the fact that while 'increased and improved options' has some objective meaning, and ascertaining it in terms of greater or less is probably possible, the more nearly final goal of autonomy, and kindred concepts, is elusive and its attainment is a matter of ever-contestable opinion.

---

[1] In a particularly convoluted version, 'negative' freedom is instrumental and 'is valuable inasmuch as it serves positive freedom', while positive freedom is, in turn, instrumental for the higher goal of 'autonomy'. (*Cf.* J. Raz, *The Morality of Freedom*, Oxford: OUP, 1986, pp. 409-10.)

[2] *Ibid.*   [3] *Ibid.*

[4] Raz, *op. cit.*, p. 416.   [5] Raz, *op. cit.*, p. 425.

In sum, the insertion of 'positive freedom' as a liberal goal makes the resulting political theory if anything even more like 'all things to all men' than does simple non-coercion alone.

4. Stretching the Harm Principle

(a) Legitimate Coercion

From the rôle of freedom as a maximising principle, we are now ready to move on to that of the complementary restrictive rule which formally completes the freedom-oriented theory. Until recently, one such rule was widely accepted in virtually all versions of liberalism. It is best understood as a three-part statement:

(1) freedom may be constrained only by legitimate coercion;

(2) coercing a person is legitimate if and only if it is necessary for preventing *harm to other persons*;

(3) legitimate coercion is mandatory.

Obviously, (1) is not controversial. Nobody would agree to freedom being illegitimately constrained. (3) follows from unconstrained freedom being potentially destructive; it is mandatory to prevent harm. Tort law, criminal law, and public order as a whole are, rightly or wrongly, thought to depend on (3) being accepted. Such problems as arise are connected with (2), the operationally significant part of the rule.

On the face of it, its classical formulation by J. S. Mill[1] does not admit of any ambiguity. He enunciates, with great clarity, the rule-principle I call *A* (below), and immediately elaborates it by adding the subsidiary rule *B* which, though implicit in the words 'to others' in *A*, might otherwise escape notice:

(*A*) '... the only purpose for which power can be rightfully exercised over any member of a civilized community, against his will, is to prevent harm to others.'

(*B*) 'His own good, either physical or moral, is not a sufficient warrant.'

---

[1] *On Liberty*, Ch. I, para. 9. The harm principle, in a less well articulated form, already makes a tentative appearance in the French revolutionary 'Declaration of the Rights of Man and of Citizens' (Article IV).

A contains the whole of the harm principle. The explanatory sub-clause *B* is contained in *A*, and in strict logic need not have been separately stated. However, it does throw a stronger light on an aspect of the principle, anti-paternalism and anti-moralism, that used to raise controversy (and still does). The major thrust of the principle, however, asserts not that his own good is *not* a proper ground for coercing a person, but that harm to others *is*, and that it is the *sole* ground.

The ordinary application of this is, and has been for more than a century, that the state has the duty to stop its subjects from burning each other's hayricks (thought it must allow them to burn their own). It *must* prevent anyone causing wilful damage to another's life, limb and property, but *may not* interfere with 'liberty and property' to promote any other end. To achieve this, it must ensure external security and civil order, administering the commutative justice that sanctions its disturbance. Such a limited rôle for the state is, in fact, easily derived from Hobbes's conception, where the state's mandate is first and last a protective one, though absolute at that. Some caricatures, drawn with little talent, mock this as the puny 'nightwatchman' state, others as the all-devouring Leviathan. Both caricatures are missing much of the point.

Classical liberalism has spelt out, less cryptically than Hobbes had done two centuries earlier, the nature of the only mandate a government can honestly claim to have if it purports to hold it by some, perhaps unsaid, but potentially unanimous free consent of the governed. There is no possible provision in a potentially unanimous mandate for disposing of people or their resources for any purpose other than to stop them from harming each other.

It is of course perfectly possible to disagree with Hobbes's philosophy of the state, or with the requirement of unanimity (if only potentially), or for that matter with classical liberalism as a whole for its dependence on the harm principle. What does not seem possible is for reasonable men to deny that the latter is a *complete* principle encompassing every possible case without exception. It divides every possible action of the government into two classes: one which it *must* and the other which it *may not* do. It excludes any 'middle', leaving no discernible area between the two where there would be room for discretionary activism upon selected targets.

(b) An Indeterminate Middle

Some recent liberal writers are nevertheless persuaded that they see a discretionary middle, and a vast one at that. In an astonishing declaration delivered with much assurance, Ronald Dworkin affirms that the harm principle, far from being all-encompassing, 'speaks only to those *relatively rare* occasions'[1] where an act is at least potentially harmful to its actor, or harmless to him but morally offensive to others. Its relevance is to 'driving a motorcycle without a helmet', to homosexuality, drug taking or pornography, in sum a not wholly unimportant but certainly peripheral part of a government's business. The central part it does not address at all. It 'says nothing about how government shall distribute scarce resources like income',[2] and similar issues of great social or economic importance.

On any reading of Mill's statement above, the main thesis *A* speaks audibly enough to the last point, even if (as we shall see in (c) and (d) below) there may be divided opinions about how broadly or how narrowly one should interpret its command. The original reading, which is still fairly standard, is that the government shall *not* 'distribute scarce resources like income' because incomes belong to their recipients who earn them or have other lawful title to them. Nothing supports the tacit assumption, made by many modern liberals despite its inconsistency with liberal individualism, that it is somehow the prerogative of the state to 'distribute resources'.

Before assuming this, one would have to explain why the resources in question do *not* belong to the individuals who acquired, earned, saved or inherited them. Socialists do, but liberals do not offer such an explanation. Instead, if anything is said at all, it is intimated that, although individuals *do* have property rights in resources, 'society' has an *overriding say* in their exercise. (We shall examine this position in Part Two, Chapter 5.) In keeping with the injunction of the harm principle, the government may commandeer some of the income its subjects produce for themselves if, but only if, this is necessary for preventing them from harming one another. The occasion for

---

[1] R. Dworkin, *Taking Rights Seriously*, London: Duckworth, 1977, quotations from 5th impression, 1987, p. 261 (my italics).

[2] *Ibid.*

this is implicit in the harm principle. It is when resources must be diverted to the government's mandatory production of the harm-preventing, 'protective' public goods of order and peace.

Once again, it is possible to disagree with this reading of the harm principle, as it is to reject it altogether. But it is preposterous to pretend that it 'says nothing' about 'how the government shall distribute scarce resources'. It proposes a complete rule to regulate it, allowing no gaps, no unprovided-for cases left to one's discretion. Rebelling against its restrictive discipline, some liberals are moved to recapture discretion. They re-interpret 'harm' to fill the rule with a new, wider content they believe morally superior or permitting better policies. The result is a more flexible, discretionary version of liberalism. These attempts at re-interpretation are at least straight and above board. We shall examine some presently.

Dworkin's stratagem, however, is of a different order. Because of the popular appeal of his views, it is worth looking at in detail. He takes the sub-clause *B* as if it stood alone and simply disregards *A*, the principle itself. It is a puzzle why he thinks he can do this. With a little goodwill, however, one can read a reason, albeit a lame one, into his text. He states, cryptically, that no principle can conclusively settle more than a few 'relatively rare' issues. For, or so he explains, it is a 'blunder' to confuse the 'force of a principle with its range'.[1] The ballistic metaphor is no more persuasive than most other metaphors. Yet it is meant to persuade us that if we wish to avoid blunder, we must not read the harm principle as it is written. We are to understand that its 'range' *must* be limited to non-paternalism, legal moralism and victimless crimes, because if it were not so limited, it would not have enough 'force'.

Why anyone should believe that, contrary to ballistics, there must be an inverse relation (or any relation at all) between the range and the force of a principle, remains unrevealed. If anything, it looks less contrived to suppose that the greater is the force, the longer will be its range. Since, however, he 'limits the range' of the harm principle to peripheral 'harm-to-oneself'

---

[1] Dworkin, *op. cit.*, p. 260. It is of this 'blunder' that he condemns Gertrude Himmelfarb, a distinguished scholar of 19th-century political thought—a blunder from which her argument 'does not recover'.

issues, Dworkin permits himself to believe that it leaves, between 'must' and 'may not', a wide middle ground beyond the principle's 'range' where government carries out its main business, notably the 'distribution of scarce resources', either on a pragmatic and discretionary basis, or guided by rules *other than* the harm principle. This allows Dworkin's preferred alternative rule, equality, to hold sway.

(c) Harm and Wrongful Harm

There are straighter and intellectually more solid attempts, too, at getting the harm principle to say that the proper function of government does not stop at ensuring order and commutative justice. Instead of pretending that the harm principle does not cover issues going much beyond seat-belts and the display of homosexuality, they adopt interpretations that are formally coherent and involve no deceitful claims.

The concept of harm is inevitably moral and evaluative. Statements about its meaning are neither true nor false. One can maintain that its proper understanding is to confine it to wrongful damage to an interest, where 'wrongful' is meant much as the common law understands tort. It is this interpretation of the harm principle that inspired liberalism through most of the 19th century. The firmness of 'wrongful' came from the anchor that tied it to a corpus of established legal rules and precedents whose existence and content were matters of record, knowable within tolerably narrow limits. The common law meaning of wrongful may not be crystal clear in every case, but in most cases there is a mass of accumulated evidence about it, and a widely agreed procedure, the trial, for testing contested meanings. As long as the harm principle was supposed to derive its precise sense from such a body of common knowledge—a sense akin to the legal-positivist one of unlawful—its guidance about what the state must or must not do to limit freedom was firm and unambiguous.

In contrast to the positive meaning, normative meanings of wrongful are derived from natural law, moral law (though the two are often regarded as identical), or less ambitiously from the *ad hoc* intuitions of the observer of particular cases. By their nature, they are untestable. However inspiring and appealing, they have the status of *opinions*. It would be distorting their features to say that they serve as a moral umbrella under which 'anything goes', for however subjective these opinions may be, truly outlandish notions of wrongful harm would not stand up[1] under them. But even short of the absurd, the normative meaning is flexible enough to justify a wide variety of purportedly harm-preventing coercive measures.

Many if not most harms done by people to other people or their interests are the inevitable and possibly quite unintentional consequences of scarcity, finiteness, crowdedness, specificity. What I own you cannot own, where I come first you can at best come second, if I cut down my tree you cannot enjoy its shade. These are facts of life and the state is not, under the harm principle, mandated to ban them, nor help the victim get compensation from the perpetrator if they do occur all the same. All these 'rightful' harms fall under the vast category that the common law treats as non-compensable damages *(damnum absque injuria)*[2] which we either have to put up with as the price of living in society, or buy protection from by negotiating contracts of immunity with the perpetrators. Either way, the argument about the state's duty is closed. When, however, the ground for not interfering with individuals' freely chosen actions is held to be that

> 'no plausibly interpreted harm principle could support the prohibition of actions that cause harms without violating rights',[3]

a whole new dimension opens up, where controversy and creative thought about who has and *who ought to have what rights*, finds ample scope.

The rising preoccupation with rights is a critically important aspect of the fission of liberal theory. It is considered in Chapter 3. Suffice it to say here that if the creation of rights—or, as some would put it, the translation of moral rights into legal ones—is a prerogative or indeed a duty of the state, by multiplying rights the state will vastly expand the domain where the harm principle

---

[1] However, many judgements, and damages awarded, in American product liability, medical malpractice, negligence and accident cases, raise the question of where commonsense stops and the truly outlandish begins.

[2] R. A. Epstein, *Takings: Private Property and the Power of Eminent Domain*, Cambridge, Mass.: Harvard University Press, 1985, p. 340 n.

[3] J. Feinberg, *Harm to Others*, New York: OUP, 1984, p. 36.

requires it to act. The reason is simply that facts-of-life type harms which it *may not* suppress by coercion, will be re-classified as rights-violating harms which it *must* prohibit. Working backwards from coercive measures, rights can be discovered to justify them.

(d) Externalities

When harm need no longer be wrongful in the common law sense to constitute a valid ground for forcing people to do what they would not otherwise have done, or interdicting what they would have done, the guidance of the harm principle acts in the opposite way from the original intention that first inspired it. It becomes a goad to state action rather than a curb, as it was meant to be. This is the case when the principle is completely generalised and the myriads of negative externalities, that are the unwelcome by-products of dense populations busily going about their daily business, all become *potential grounds* for invoking the harm principle.

It seems altogether reasonable to say that if it is meant to constrain people's dangerous freedom to harm one another, it should be applied irrespective of whether the harm it prevents is intentional or not. Intent or malice should at best count as one of the considerations in selecting the harms people ought to be protected against. The victim's interest, and no doubt his identity (whether he is weak or strong, defenceless or self-reliant), should weigh as heavily. *Externalities are those consequences which,* even if foreseen, *do not enter into the motivation of the actions that cause them.* By definition, such consequences are external to the actor: they do not affect him and touch only others. The manufacturer of chemicals lets noxious fumes into the air because this is part of his most economical process of concocting his product. He gets no wicked satisfaction from poisoning the neighbourhood downwind from him. However, a generalised harm principle can hardly leave him free to adopt such a process. This conclusion may be in doubt if the downwind residents have no legal claim to immunity from fumes, but springs into place the instant a 'right to clean air' is discovered.

Like many reasonable and seemingly innocuous propositions that seem almost impossible and certainly churlish to disagree with, such an extension of the harm principle has effects we do not anticipate when we first cheer it on its way. Basically, it shifts the justificatory, legitimising ground of the coercive restriction of freedom. Instead of the *wrongfulness* of the action of the perpetrator, it is the *interest* of the victim that legitimises interference. Consequently, *suffering* from a state of affairs can be an adequate warrant for claiming *remedy* under the harm principle, without having to show that the state of affairs was brought about by somebody's wrongful action.

In the case of pollution, this has a certain plausibility. It accords with the spirit of the age to assign liability to the manufacturer for emitting noxious fumes even if his adoption of the particular process of production was lawful at the time. But the same reasoning would equally well justify, for example, the re-introduction of the medieval sumptuary laws for keeping expenditure within seemly bounds, to curb the ostentation of the rich which makes the poor's poverty harder to bear. Coming back full circle in the name of the arch-liberal harm principle to the restrictions of a pre-liberal age would be ironical, yet the prospect is not wholly fanciful. It would fit into the evolution of liberal theory along the line of least resistance, left open by the looseness of its structure.

Marrying up the harm principle with externalities produces a fertile paradigm, spurring on the formulation of policies that call for more legitimate coercion. For, despite rigorous refutations,[1] externalities for educated public opinion remain stubbornly associated with the idea of an inefficient and unfair divergence between social and private cost, social and private benefit. As such, they are seen as symptoms of 'market failure'. It is incumbent upon a government to step in and rectify such failures either by taxes and subsidies, or by prohibitions, whichever is better suited to the case.

Correcting 'market failure' is characteristically liberal in that it is *meliorist*—it sets out to fix something because it believes it could be made to work better. Yet it contributes neither to the maximisation of freedom in any obvious way, nor to the formation of undisputable constraints within which it is to be

---

[1] The classic text is R. H. Coase, 'The Problem of Social Cost', *Journal of Law and Economics*, 1960. *Cf.* S. N. S. Cheung, *The Myth of Social Cost*, Hobart Paper 78, London: Institute of Economic Affairs, 1978, especially J. Burton's 'Epilogue' to Cheung's text.

carried out. Nevertheless, when leaning upon the harm principle in the rôle of the one-by-one spotter and the scourge of negative externalities, the state can be represented as the patient and relentless minimiser of all the harm that freedom would otherwise do.

(e) Failing to Do Good

The ultimate step in escalating the harm principle—there is no other, more radical one in sight—is to conflate 'harming' with 'not helping'.

The step begins, reasonably enough, with establishing the duty of succour even bad Samaritans owe to fellow human beings in jeopardy. When the succour is not onerous and the jeopardy is grave, the duty to aid is hardly in dispute. There is a measure of agreement that it should be enforced by coercion if need be. However, 'onerous' and 'grave' are, with 'acceptable', 'real', 'significant', and so on, politically pliable, twistable words, and it is always a source of contestation if an important criterion must totally depend on such words. Where, faced with another's 'grave' need, a person's enforceable duty begins, and how 'onerous' it must be before he is relieved of it,[1] comes ultimately to depend on the climate of opinion, itself conditioned by vested interests and demands.

The régime of welfare entitlements, and of the matching taxes, will be that which is electorally most suitable, best adjusted to that climate. Such a régime of succour tends to expand, due to the superficially correct belief of each interest group pressing for a welfare benefit or a fiscal favour, that what it obtains will mostly be paid for by other groups. The mechanism has been amply explored by public-choice theory over the last two or three decades. Luckily for the justifier, the justification of this régime by liberal ideology can be derived from the harm principle—a more characteristically liberal ground than such alternatives as 'equality' or 'distributive justice', norms that liberals must, sometimes uneasily, share with socialists.

At this point, we can look back in wonder on the way the harm principle has changed its content since it was first adopted as

---

[1] On the 'where-to-draw-the-line' problem, *cf.* Feinberg, *op. cit.*, pp. 150-63. See also his subtle discussion of the causation of harm in Ch. 4.

perhaps the key rule of liberalism. Starting from 'wrongful action damaging the interest of another', it stretched over 'negative externality', potentially bringing under its scope most of the ordinary business of life. There was a concomitant widening of the responsibility for harm. From 'causing' harm, responsibility has expanded to 'having it in one's power to make it cease'. Nor could the set of coercive measures required to give effect to so broad a principle remain confined to the *suppression* of wrongful-and-harmful acts. It, too, expanded and can now *require* the performance of acts *beneficial to others* though *costly to oneself.*

Pushed to the limit, forbearing from doing good may mean doing harm. Whether it does, calling for the coerced doing of good, is ultimately a political decision. It is so by default, for the simple reason that no other authority, moral or otherwise, is invested with the competence conclusively to decide it. Confirmation of this reading is provided by the curiously tentative, permissive formulation of Raz, usually a most acute and precise legal and political philosopher:

> '*Sometimes* failing to improve the situation of another is harming him . . . the harm principle *allows* [the government] to force [some of its subjects] to take actions which are required to improve people's options and opportunities[1] . . . It follows that a government is *entitled* to redistribute resources, to provide public goods and . . . other services on a compulsory basis.'[2]

Lest it should swallow up all of social life and require the application of coercion to every conceivable human action save the absolutely neutral ones—if there are any such—the harm principle in this version is restated in the permissive mode. It is no longer *mandatory* for the state to suppress an action that would harm another, nor to force the doing of good every time that this would improve the options of others. The state is now 'allowed', and 'entitled', to do these things *sometimes.* Failing a more precise, more rigorous mandate provided by a firmer principle, the government has *de facto* and *de jure* discretion to apply coercion in every case where in its wisdom it judges that *not* applying the resources of some to the benefit of others would be harming them.

---

[1] Raz, *op. cit.*, p. 416 (my italics).

[2] *Ibid.*, p. 417 (my italics).

While the government has discretion in the matter, its subjects have a duty to submit when it chooses to exercise it. Under the expanded harm principle, not only is everybody his brother's keeper, but the brother has, by and large, a valid claim to be kept.

If one's obligation to keep and the other's correlative right to be kept, were definite, the government would have no discretion in the matter but would have to enforce the right. This would of course lead to absurd results in practice. However, the government's discretion has an interesting consequence: the system of rights becomes more fluid, more a matter of almost day-to-day politics. The selective recognition of some rights moves to the centre of the liberal political order.

3

RIGHTS

1. Rights-Liberalism

PERHAPS THE most telling mark of the current liberal vocabulary is the frequency of the words 'right' and 'rights'. Rights are agreeable, reassuring, beneficial to the right-holder, morally or materially valuable. It is not immediately obvious whether they cost anything. Perhaps they are the 'free lunch' *par excellence* and need only to be recognised in order to be enjoyed. A position that is 'against rights' would hardly be tenable; to be 'for rights' is to be in sympathy with the general aspirations of mankind. Securing men and women in their rights is confirming them in what they ought to have.

It is only natural that political theories, and the parties, groups or movements by and large identified with them, have taken to rights and to rights-talk with mounting enthusiasm. They keep proclaiming lists of human rights, civil rights, minority rights, women's rights, 'economic and social rights', rights to education, employment, opportunity and security, 'democratic' rights, 'development rights', cultural rights and many other rights whose exact meaning and practical effect are far from being always evident.

Liberalism has stayed ahead of the pack in this respect. It had from the beginning a basic disposition favourable to rights whose subjects are primarily (though not necessarily) individuals, and hence fewer inhibitions about espousing most of them than rival currents of political thought that had class, nation, race or community, rather than the right-holding person, as their central interest. The liberal emphasis on rights—in some authors a repetitive preoccupation with them—leads to entire theories being understood as 'rights-based' (in opposition to 'goal-based').[1] The word may be intended to convey that it takes the existence of certain rights as its first principles, not deriving them from God's will, the essence of human nature, the conditions of wellbeing or anything else; its rights require neither verification in a positive, nor justification in a normative, sense.

The rest of the theory is then constructed around these rights, which must if possible be bolstered and at all events not be contradicted by it. Thus the very first sentence of Nozick's theory of the state[2] simply declares that 'Individuals have rights' without seeking to show why ever they should. They have rights in a general way. Any specific ones they have enable them to acquire others, individually by contract, or collectively through their influence on legislation. The former is principally to create and transfer property rights; the latter is the father of all collectively generated rights and obligations. The prior entitlement of all to some rights to begin with is offered as a self-evident truth. Thus an axiomatic starting-point is provided, from which the shape of a political order compatible with these rights can be deduced. One weakness of taking this road is that rights are not the most suitable candidates for the rôle of self-evident truths. On the whole, some other starting-point than the kind taken by Nozick might help to make the axiomatic treatment of liberalism (or libertarianism) less vulnerable to sceptical criticism.

Another possible form of a 'rights-based' theory would postulate that the political order has, as its principal function (to which any others must be subordinated), the creation and enforcement of certain rights we judge that people *ought* to have. The theory of a pure *Rechtsstaat*, a state whose overriding purpose is to uphold the rule of law, would be a rights-based theory of this form. It is in this form, too, that modern liberalism is rights-based.

As such, however, it ceases to be a specifically liberal political theory, for it is detached from any substantive relation to the

---

[1] Dworkin, *op. cit.*, Ch. 6.

[2] R. Nozick, *Anarchy, State, Utopia*, New York: Basic Books, 1974, p. ix.

object of securing and enhancing freedom. The latter may happen to be a by-product of a system of rights. But rights as such do not necessarily favour freedom before other desirable features of social relations. Indeed, if being liberal calls for some kind of priority rank for freedom among other goods, the rights-based version of liberalism is misnamed. Current usage, however, is above such terminological quibbles. Albeit with misgivings, I will conform to it in what follows.

Giving rights pride of place is an undertaking full of built-in difficulties or, as a now unfashionable parlance used to put it, 'internal contradictions'. If it can be carried off at all, then only in a loose, incompletely defined form that permits it to be invested with a variety of mutually antagonistic content.

Every meaningful right, that is, every right that is more than empty rhetoric and carries potentially valuable practical consequences, involves a relation between two persons (or groups of persons, or legal entities): the right-holder and another. The benefit the right secures for the right-holder has, as its mirror image, the obligation of at least one other person to perform the act conferring the benefit, or to refrain from acts that would diminish it. Creating rights means[1] creating obligations that must either be discharged or remain outstanding.

A straightforward maximising principle—'the more rights to the more people, the better'—has as its inseparable corollary the *maximisation of obligations.* Plainly, however, 'the more

---

[1] It has been suggested that stating a right is not logically equivalent to stating the corresponding obligation—that, in fact, no obligation need correspond to the right and it is possible to create a right without creating any obligation. (*Cf.* J. Waldron, *The Right to Private Property*, Oxford: OUP, 1988, pp. 68-69.) Two possibilities are cited in support:

(a) Legislation assigns a right to (a class of) persons without, for the time being, assigning to anybody a correlative obligation. This alleged possibility is not one. The legislator, seeking to confer a right, can defer assigning the obligation, but as long as he does, the right is in abeyance. He has made a promise of a future right instead of conferring one now.

(b) A right is created, or the existence of a hitherto latent one is recognised, by the legislator or judge. The existence of an obligation is then derived from this recognition. This is obviously possible, but does not affect the fact that the *exercise* of the right presupposes that somebody else is honouring a correlative obligation. This presupposition is a valid one regardless of whether the recognition of the right by the legislator *caused* him to impose the obligation.

obligations upon the more people, the worse it is', for while only some obligations are onerous and others can be honoured without significant cost in terms of resources, effort, inconvenience or self-denial, none are positively agreeable to bear. 'Rights-maximisation', even if it has an intelligible meaning other than the sheer affirmation of the greatest possible number of rights to which the greatest number of persons are entitled, could therefore never pass for an unqualified, self-evidently desirable objective of a political order.

Anticipating strands of argument that will be deployed presently, one may tentatively conclude that rights-liberalism is either a gross mistake of reasoning and should be dismissed, or it depends on an 'on balance' type of evaluation: the rights we ask the political process to recognise or 'create' are, on balance, worth more to the moral order of the world, or do more for the wellbeing of the beneficiaries, than the material burden or loss of autonomy of action we would thus impose on those who must be made to bear the matching obligations.

This type of evaluation judges political choices by their consequences. It is characteristic of the utilitarian tradition, and as such it is explicitly abjured by most rights-liberals who tend vigorously to protest against the least suspicion of being consequentialists and allowing one man to be used as the instrument of the 'greater' good of others. One of the 'internal contradictions' of rights-liberalism, in other words, is that the 'rights-based' theory crucially depends on the consequentialist argument that the benefits conferred by the development of its system of rights somehow *outweigh* the burdens imposed by the corresponding extension of obligations.

2. Rights as Ramparts

In Chapter 2 it was argued that a maximisation postulate (e.g. 'maximise freedom!') must pull in double harness with a regulating principle, a rule that will constrain the *maximand* within some chosen channel, corridor or, more likely, maze. The harm principle could serve as such a rule in that it defines, without remainder, when coercion may not and when it must be applied to restrict freedom. It is the classic example of a complete rule. However, though complete, it is elastic. In usage it proves ambiguous, twistable, and stretches unconscionably. The latter property does not mean at all that it reduces legitimate coercion to an unduly small rôle, nor that it fails to give any guidance on the government's main business and notably on what it may or may not do about scarce resources. It means, on the contrary, that as it identifies more and more harms (including under 'harms' the *lack of benefits and opportunities*) against which its subjects must be protected, the government makes more and more aspects of life its business. As the concept of harm expands, the domain over which coercion must, or at least 'may', be applied expands with it, until we realise that the harm principle has become a sort of ventriloquist's doll, capable of rendering one political agenda as well as any other.

In its place, rights-liberalism inserts an inventory of separately enumerated rights that all persons belonging to defined categories are deemed to have. Each right is meant to be a rampart, protecting the corresponding interest of the individual right-holder against any encroaching purpose, including the purposes of the entire political community. Outside them, in the no man's land, however, the community's overall goal may still be maximised subject, as it were, to its not breaching any rampart. Within the ramparts, individual interests have priority over the common goal; outside them it is the other way round.[1] The common goal may be any *maximand*—'utility', the gross domestic product, 'equality' or the flowering of the arts. It may be freedom, too, though (as we had occasion to observe earlier) modern rights-liberalism does not single out freedom for specially favourable attention.[2]

---

[1] Gently berating Mill for supposing a harmony between basic individual rights and overall utility, Herbert Hart states:

'. . . in the last resort, there is an unbridgeable gap between . . . maximisation of the total aggregate general welfare or happiness . . . and principles protecting . . . certain aspects of individual welfare and recognizing these as constraints on the maximizing aggregative principle.' (H. L. A. Hart, *Essays in Jurisprudence and Philosophy*, Oxford: OUP, 1983, p. 188.)

On the face of it the gap need not be unbridgeable. It *need* not even exist. For there is nothing formally wrong with putting a *maximand* under some constraint that stops it from expanding in a particular direction. As usual, however, Hart is nevertheless right, for rights prove to be untrustworthy in the rôle of constraints.

[2] For Dworkin, for example, 'we can maintain [the idea that men and women have a right to it] only by so watering down the idea of a right that the right to
[*Contd. on p. 38*]

The manifestoes of rights-liberals are Bills of Rights, Declarations of Human Rights, Covenants, Conventions for the respect of certain general rights. Many of these acts and documents have a definite legal status; far from being mere wish-lists, unilateral pretensions, some are binding in intent and pass for constitutional or international law. They are increasingly elaborate, running to dozens of articles, most of which assert entitlements to many benefits, and providing in some cases for rights of exquisite thoughtfulness. One assures the 'free develop-ment of one's personality', another the 'continuous improvement of living conditions', and a third the 'enjoyment of the arts'. It is not totally clear who is obligated to see to it that the right to develop one's personality, or to enjoy the arts, can in fact be exercised, and to what extent. In this, however, recent rights-lists are no more surrealist and light of touch than their more concise predecessors which, with restraint and simplicity, confined themselves, for example, to 'life, liberty and the pursuit of happiness'.

If all these rights are ramparts, both securing people in the possession of what they have and reserving for them what they might not otherwise have, it is predictable that as time goes on and eyes are opened, society is destined to have more and more of them, behind which more and more of our particular interests are sheltered. If the realisation of a common goal must not involve trespass, but shall instead tiptoe around in the pro-gressively more restricted no man's land outside the ramparts, rights-liberalism progresses, too, towards the gradual denial of collective purposes.

This may not, in itself, be a cause for alarm. Most collective purposes are only too apt to look out for themselves. But their negation, salutary as it may be much of the time, sits ill with another, equally pronounced bias of the modern evolution of liberal thought. This is its growing readiness to subordinate individual convenience, preference and the very rights that are supposed to stand as their ramparts, giving priority over them to

---

liberty is something hardly worth having at all ... I would therefore not recognize the claim that some men and women want liberty as requiring any compromise in the efforts that I believe are necessary to give other men and women the equality to which they are entitled.' (Dworkin, *op. cit.*, p. 268.)

'socially agreed' values—that is, to equality in its diverse guises, or to 'distributive justice'. Often, individual right is simply to give way to 'the public interest', to the 'balance of benefit', as seen by men of goodwill and good sense, or as decreed in the political process. The former is as intellectual élites would have it, the latter as majoritarian democrats, but either way the priority of rights ceases to be a *rule* and becomes a matter of *discretion.*

The apparent contradiction with the ostensible agenda of rights-liberalism, to the extent that it is resolved, merely shows that, contrary to the phrase that has lately been fashionable, rights are not 'trumps'. Dworkin's real thesis is that they are, but only *up to a point*:

> 'Individual rights are political trumps held by individuals. Individuals have rights when, for some reason, a collective goal is not sufficient justification for denying them ...'[1]

But even a fundamental moral right can be overridden 'to obtain a clear and major public benefit'.[2] A right 'has a threshold weight against collective goals in general'[3] and may have to yield 'to an urgent policy with which it competes ...'.[4]

Rights rest on distributional principles; such principles compete with collective goals:

> '... offering less of some benefits to one man can be justified *simply by showing* that this will lead to a greater benefit overall'.[5]

> 'No one has a political right ... unless the reasons for giving him what he asks are stronger than some collective justification.'[6]

In brief, it all depends on *which* reason weighs more. But what is the good of enunciating that the heavier weight outweighs the lighter one and it all depends on which is which? Manifestly, 'rights are trumps' when the balance of benefit does not outweigh them; they are not trumps when it does. But this is saying nothing more than that a card may be stronger than some

---

[1] Dworkin, *op. cit.*, p. xi.
[2] *Ibid.*, p. 191.
[3] *Ibid.*, p. 92.
[4] *Ibid.*
[5] *Ibid.*, p. 91 (my italics).
[6] *Ibid.*, p. 365 (my italics).

other card yet weaker than a third one. It is *not* saying that the card is a trump.[1]

Some rights may consequently prevail over some collective purpose some of the time. Nothing more predictable and absolute (i.e. rule-like) can plausibly be read into rights-liberalism.

It is fairly evident, too, that in this spirit the more luxuriously rights proliferate, the more often they will fail to prevail over the collective will, acting through the very government which is meant to enforce their non-violation. Unsurprisingly, the inflation of rights devalues them, and the enterprise of basing a political order on the recognition of an ever richer and fuller system of rights proves to be self-defeating.

3. Rights That Are Wrongs

The truth of the matter seems to be that, for rights-liberalism, rights are not primarily ramparts sheltering something we have anyway but want to protect. Their rôle is only secondarily to protect individual goals and achievements from the antagonistic interests of some other individuals or of the whole collectivity. They *are* the goals to be achieved. In this variety of loose liberalism, the dual structure—a maximisation postulate constrained by a rule—is effectively replaced by what looks like a unitary structure, the constraint-less maximisation of an objective that, for lack of a more precise term, could be called the 'sum of everyone's rights'. Such a sum cries out loud to be dismissed as

---

[1] A 'trump' is an absolute right which defeats non-trumps (collective goals) and can be defeated only by a higher trump (another absolute right). This is the only sense of 'trump' that could make Dworkin's thesis non-empty and worth putting forward. But no right he calls 'concrete' (protecting someone's specific benefit) is ever absolute in the political theory within which he conducts his arguments (*cf.* the quotes above). His non-concrete right to 'equal concern and respect' is intended to be absolute. Whether it is or not is immaterial to the present issue, for it cannot be changed into the coin of 'concrete' rights. 'Equal concern and respect' is devoid of any specific meaning that would make it compelling for reasonable men to agree, with respect to how people are treated in a given situation, either that it is violated or that it is not. (Anyone who finds this statement surprising should experiment with arguments for and against compulsory busing of schoolchildren to achieve racially mixed school populations. Are the children being bused treated with the *same* concern and respect as those being bused to?)

meaningless, but I believe it would be better to bear with it for a moment, for it repays study.

There is in contemporary political discourse, as we had occasion to note, a groundswell of assertions, declarations and claims about a lengthening list of rights people are purported to have or ought to have. In many cases, the claim that a certain moral right exists and ought to be given recognition in law is merely the translation of a collective purpose into individual rights-talk. Thus rights to equal chances, 'level playing fields', equality of status and material condition, palatable options, autonomy, security of livelihood and so forth, are broadly taken care of by the collective goal of an equal distribution, though the former express the latter in a more elaborate and perhaps more appealing guise. Likewise, the lists of rights to many different 'freedoms' could really be subsumed, without much distortion or loss of content, under freedom as the general objective, to be pursued in choosing social institutions and arrangements. However, if over wide fields of subject matter, stating collective goals and individual rights are two ways of saying much the same thing, there must be some advantage in resorting to rights-talk. Otherwise it is hard to account for the recent tidal wave of rights-claims and proclamations.

One possible reason is that this way of putting things fits the individualism that, though no longer in very good repair, is still the natural habitat of most liberal thinkers. Another may have to do with some unconscious, 'natural' selection of ideals. 'Rights' survive and crowd 'goals' out of circulation even if both convey the same substantive message, because rights-talk cheers and gratifies all who are accorded rights by it, and threatens no one overtly. Goals, on the other hand, unless they are innocuous, usually suggest not only the promise of something beneficial, but also the cost of attaining it, the effort it takes, and sometimes (in the case of visibly redistributive goals) an implication that if some gain by it, others must lose. Rights-as-goals are presumably easier to propagate and fitter to survive in the public consciousness than goals *tout court*.

One after another, common goals are thus transformed into the rights we ought to possess as members of the polity. As their list gets longer and fuller, it is the good life that is taking shape under our eyes:

'When we survey this list, we realize [that it] is simply a way of sketching the *outlines of the common good*' [and once the outline is rounded out] 'there is no room left for an appeal, *against* the exercise of these rights, to "general welfare".'[1]

Nor, for that matter, would the opposite appeal make any sense: these rights are not ramparts to protect the individual's interest against the claims of general welfare, for they *are* the general welfare. Imprecisely but without any prospect of a more precise rival, they are the universal, composite *maximand* the political authority in the liberal state should pursue. This position, put by Finnis with clarity and force, is probably the sole coherent way to account for the rôle that rights really play in rights-liberalism.

Does such an account allow us to understand it as a firm doctrine, offering predictable guidance, and suffering from no self-contradiction?

It bears repetition, and perhaps cannot even be repeated often enough, that one person's right is the obligation of another. In any 'closed set'—and although a society is never quite closed to other societies, it is as a rule not heavily parasitic on another, and enjoys no major benefits whose costs it does not have to bear— adding rights *means* adding obligations. Rights are agreeable, obligations are not. By the most elementary kind of calculus, 'maximising rights' cannot possibly be a generally acceptable goal for the set, that is, one whose achievement everybody in it either welcomes or is at worst indifferent to. Adding to their obligations may harm some of them and can at best leave the rest indifferent.

At some point, therefore, an 'impartial observer' may very well judge that certain rights are wrongs, and that maximising rights is an altogether mistaken objective from a moral or a practical point of view (assuming these are separate considerations). Less impartial ones are liable to come to one of two possible judgements. Either they welcome rights-maximisation because it adds to their rights and to the obligations of others. Or they deplore it, holding that deliberately adding to the obligations one

---

[1] J. Finnis, *Natural Law and Natural Right*, Oxford: OUP, 1980, p. 214 (italics in original).

already has, can only be wrong unless it is done voluntarily by the bearer of the obligation himself.

Multiplying rights can be a unanimously approved objective, but only in an 'open set' whose members can expect to shift the matching obligations to others outside their set. Within a society, there are many such open sets which, in claiming rights, can confidently hope to exploit the rest of society. Welfare rights, the rights of organised labour, rights to tariff protection, 'fair trade', 'fair prices', 'stable markets', and so on, all derive their charm from the cost being shifted outside the set of beneficiaries. But even when the shift is in large part illusory, rights that appear to cost nothing to the right-holders are tempting to have. This is what gives such forceful appeal to assertions, many of which may be true yet misleading, that we have certain rights 'against the state'[1]—for example, the right to 'equal' education—by virtue of 'judgement about what is right or wrong for governments to do'.[2] 'We' enjoy the right, the state bears the obligation: the deal is impossible to refuse.

The illusion of net gain for 'us' lingers on, thanks to the 'weasel-word' nature of the formulation, even as political sophistication spreads and 'we' admit, when pressed, that no obligation of the state will be honoured unless 'we', or some of us, are made to bear its cost.

I need not rub in the point any further. Ultimately, any change in rights brought about by 'collective choice', that is to say, by the political process rather than by contractual exchanges, is redistributive. This is true not only in the obvious case of welfare rights and rights protecting monopolies, but less obviously also in the case of 'political rights' and 'civil rights'. (Consider the cost to society of developing the rights of the accused in criminal trials, especially in the United States.) For rights-creation to be 'good', the redistribution of liabilities and resources involved must also be 'good'. To set up the fullest development of a system of rights as the political goal is tantamount to claiming that we know how to strike the balance between the advantage of those who get the rights and the burden of those who must assume the obligation. Pretending that the two sets of people are the same, and gain and

---

[1] Dworkin, *op. cit.*, p. 138.   [2] *Ibid.*, p. 139.

lose in the same proportions, is unworldly, or not meant to be taken seriously.

It is of course one thing for the liberal advocate of a certain extension of rights—for instance, the right of all to a longer and more costly public education, or to a minimum income—to hold that to men of goodwill, the gain to the poor and the insecure must outweigh the loss to the better-off who will finance it. Such claims *on behalf of others*, by appeal to moral sentiments, are the expressions of some moral preference. Pressure-group claims for resources on their *own behalf* express some material interest. Both are coherent, and can compete with rival moral preferences or material interests, with the chips falling where they may. It is, however, quite another thing for the same liberal advocate to affect to *know* that the gain does, as a matter of conceivably ascertainable fact, outweigh the loss.

That kind of claim, a hangover from the early utilitarian associations of liberalism, and hence anathema to modern rights-liberalism that prohibits using one person as a means to the good of another, is now widely regarded as nonsensical. The same Finnis who sees rights as the cumulative building blocks of the common good, nevertheless states:

'[No] plausible sense can be given . . . to the notion of a "greater net good" . . . or "greater balance of good over bad" . . . it is senseless in the way that it is senseless to sum together the size of this page, the number six, and the mass of this book.'[1]

Yet, to the discomfiture of rights-liberalism, if the balancing of the good of some against the bad of others is senseless, the extension of rights until their 'sum' maximises the common good and fulfils the purpose of the political order, is senseless too. For the road to the common good via individual rights is paved with nothing but interpersonal comparisons.

Quite likely it is impossible to accept a theory authorising any interventionist policy, without being prepared to judge the consequences 'on balance' (for few such policies bring *only* benefits to some and *no* costs to anybody). Naturally, doing so is to make interpersonal comparisons. Contemporary liberalism is

[1] Finnis, *op. cit.*, pp. 112-13.

both wedded to positive policies as 'dictated by reason', and to the refusal of the consequentialist 'on-balance' assessment of their merits. Can the contradiction be resolved?

One answer is that if one is interested in policies, one cannot refuse to consider their consequences, and if this involves compromises with the deontology of rights, one should go ahead and compromise:

> '... consequential reasoning may be fruitfully used even when consequentialism as such is not accepted. To ignore consequences is to leave an ethical story half told. Consequentialism, however, demands more than the telling of the story. It demands, in particular, that the rightness of actions be judged entirely by the goodness of consequences, and this is a demand not merely of taking consequences into account, but of ignoring everything else'.[1]

It is impossible to object to so reasonable a position. What it amounts to, however, is that one must do the best one can, *taking all things into account*. It is a position that is so pragmatic that it can confidently dispense with the guidance of any political doctrine, liberal or otherwise.

4. The Burden of Proof

(a) 'Is-rights' and 'Ought-rights'

Under the name of right and obligation, quite disparate relations between persons are lumped together, ignoring the contrasting legal and epistemological features that lend them their respective points.

Certain rights exist as a matter of empirical fact. The evidence that they do can be found in contracts, custom, customary law and statute law. Others exist, or are claimed to do, as matters of moral intuition. Their recognition does not depend on evidence; there is none. The 'evidence' that is nonetheless invoked in their support refers to insights into the essential constants of human nature, shared by all, or to moral imperatives which reasonableness or decency do not permit us to disobey.

The first category, resting upon empirical evidence, is that of

---

[1] A. K. Sen, *On Ethics and Economics*, Oxford: OUP, 1987, p. 75.

'is-rights', the second of 'ought-rights'.[1] It is the normal rôle of political theories to assert the existence of selected 'ought-rights' and to ease the way to their transfer, by legislation, judicial law-making or the practice of the executive branch of the government, to the category of 'is-rights'. (This, of course, is a different kind of passage from 'ought' to 'is' than the naturalistic fallacy natural law theorists are, often wrongly, accused of.)

Clearly, however, the fact that an is-right exists, and the fact that a moral claim made on behalf of an ought-right is a valid claim, are in different classes of 'fact'. The former is a rigorously closed class: as of today, there is only a given sum of evidence that can be discovered to support the recognition of a given list of is-rights. The class of ought-rights is, by contrast, open-ended. New ones can always be invented; the potential list of them is indefinitely long. The 'evidence' in their favour, drawn from a bottomless well of possible arguments, can be made up as the list lengthens.

One may well concede that some core of these arguments is 'true' in the sense that a moral proposition can be held to be true; and if moral relativism denies this possibility, that is one more reason for rejecting moral relativism. But around the true core, there is unlimited room for self-serving, busybody, specious or simply inconclusive arguments for ought-rights. They are inescapable in controversies both about whether certain rights ought to be recognised and about their ranking when they conflict—which the rights that are lightly created tend to do. Few collective decisions are surrounded by more abuse of good faith and honest language, 'faction' and hypocrisy. A political theory which provokes intensive rights-talk risks giving rise to a political order where the borderline between is- and ought-rights becomes

---

[1] Natural lawyers, if uneasy with the distinction, may take comfort from observing that in no wise does it imply that an 'is-right' cannot be deduced from an 'ought-right'. A right whose violation would have offended the moral convictions of generations of all reasonable men becomes an 'is-right' by custom and will no doubt be upheld by common law judges.

I have said elsewhere that to draw inferences about moral verities from the moral consensus of society is to construct ethical theory from public opinion polls. My present position above, without advocating recourse to the pollsters' questionnaires, accepts the important rôle of moral consensus, provided it is of long enough standing, consecrated by the passage of time.

a battle-line, absorbing an inordinate share of society's attention.[1] This feeds back to the theory, forcing it to 'finesse' issues, making it looser than it would in any case be.

(b) Distributive Rights, and Others

Another incidence of the burden of proof, however, is more momentous and decisive for the strictness or looseness of liberal thought. It concerns the division of rights into two kinds according to the logical order to be followed in reaching judgements upholding them. There is one class of rights whose intrinsic nature places the burden of proof on those who claim that they exist, and another where the burden of proof is on those who would assert that they do not.

The root of the difference lies in whether the right plays a distributive rôle, appropriating a benefit, reserving it for some while excluding others. (See the analysis in the Box on pp. 48-49.)

Rights in the strict sense are distributive, and consequently carry the burden of proof. They differ fundamentally from liberties and immunities, which do not. The difference is reflected in their correlative 'mirror-images'. The correlative of a right is someone else's obligation or liability, that of a liberty or immunity the *absence* of someone's conflicting or limiting right.

A 'rights-based' political theory in general, and rights-liberalism in particular, is losing determinacy and self-restraint when it loses sight of where the burden of proof lies. Liberties and immunities are supported by the basic presumption that obligation and liability require proof, their absence does not. They work as does the commonsense principle: 'everything is permitted that is not forbidden'. Enumerating human rights, civil rights, gender rights, non-white rights, animal rights or such other rights as seem important one by one, even if it confirms the believer in their existence and exhorts the transgressor to respect them, rather tends to work along the lines of the opposing principle: 'everything is forbidden that is not expressly permitted'.

Soon enough, opinion no longer dares assume that bills of

---

[1] *Cf.* the remarks in J. Gray, *Limited Government: A Positive Agenda*, Hobart Paper 113, London: Institute of Economic Affairs, 1989, p. 25, about the effect of treating such issues as abortion, or the interests of ethnic minorities, as questions of constitutional law and basic rights.

The Basic Framework
of Rights-Relations

Following (in modified form but unchanged substance) the schema that has served generations of jurists as the basic framework of rights-logic,[1] the following relations of right can obtain between two persons *A* and *B* ('persons' being understood broadly to include classes of persons similarly placed with respect to others and to the act in question) and an act *r*:

(X)   *A* is entitled (has a 'claim-right') to have *B* do *r*. He can claim or waive *B*'s obligation[2] to *r*.

(Y)   *A* is free (has the 'liberty' or, as Hohfeld called it, the 'privilege') to do *r*. *B* is not entitled to claim either that *A* should not, or that he should, do *r*.

(W)   *A* is entitled (has the 'power') by doing *r* to impose an obligation on *B*. *B* is liable to *A*'s *r*.

(Z)   *A* is not liable for (has an 'immunity' from) *B*'s *r*. *B* is not entitled, by his act *r*, to impose an obligation on *A*.

It is perhaps confusing that the four different relations should all be called rights. Hohfeld, their constructor, advised (in vain) that to avoid muddling them up, none should be so called. From here on, I propose to reserve the name 'right' for X and W (except when referring to the arguments of others who indiscriminately call all four relations 'rights').

X, the claim-right, involves a positive obligation on the part of *B* to perform an act. The basic example of X is the contract of sale, lease or debt. But, albeit less visibly, the same X-relation binds the taxpayers *B* to the tax-beneficiaries *A* who are entitled to the services the taxes must finance.

Y, the 'privilege' we have come to call liberty, is the logical implication for *A* of the absence of any person *B* who would stand in some X or W-type relation to his *r*-act. The exercise of any of *A*'s natural faculties can serve as an example. He is free to look, to come and go, to speak, to associate with others, and generally to choose from physically available alternatives, provided he does not 'bump' into a (non-physical) constraint represented by some right X or W of *B*, or by some social *convention* (*cf.* Chapter 5).

W is the power to create an obligation. In this type of relation, a superior *A* may command, by *r*, his subordinate *B* to assume some task, to work as directed. A more complex example is the state's power, by virtue of legislation *r*, to tax its subjects.

Z, the immunity, is of course simply the absence of a relevant power W.

Some of these relations may be combined. Property is both a right and a liberty. It is a combination of an X and a Y. The claim-right X is, so to speak, its bottom layer. In it originates the acquisition by *A* of the title from *B*; the latter is put under an *ad personam* obligation to *A* to transfer it. Once *B* has discharged his obligation, *A* has an *ad rem* right in the thing he has come to own. This is, as it were, the top layer. It is in the form of a Y-liberty. Possession by *A* is sufficient for a presumption that he has this liberty. It is up to the eventual challenger to prove the contrary—that is, that *A*'s property right is limited or invalidated by somebody else's X-type right. If the challenge has enough force to require *A* to defend his title, he must prove his own X-right to it. Failing successful challenge, *A* has the unlimited enjoyment of his Y-liberty, meaning essentially that he has freedom of use and of contract (i.e. including disposal).

The fundamental point that stands out from this classification is that X and W may, but *need not*, be recognised *unless an obligation or liability can be shown to exist*, while Y and Z *must be* recognised *unless an obligation or liability can be shown to exist*.

By the rules of inferring probability and its borderline version, truth, from evidence, in X and W the burden of proof is on the *beneficiary A*, while in Y and Z it is on the *challenger*. *A* is presumed *free* and *not liable* unless proved otherwise (in much the same way as he is presumed innocent unless proved guilty). This is or should be a fundamental principle of liberal philosophy. It is comforting to find that it draws its force from the rules of logical inference.

By the same token, if *A* has a right X to claim *B*'s obligation, or the power W to impose one on him, it is up to him to provide proof if challenged, or if he seeks remedy for *B*'s eventual default.

The best proof, of course, is *B*'s own contractual recognition of his obligation, or of his liability to perform it. For political doctrines that are libertarian enough to deny the necessity for statute law and the legitimacy of the state's power to impose obligations, the voluntary contractual assumption of a positive obligation is its only valid proof.

[1] W. N. Hohfeld, *Fundamental Legal Conceptions*, New Haven: Yale University Press, 1919.

[2] 'Obligation' rather than 'duty' is being used advisedly. An obligation can be waived. It is best to reserve 'duty' for denoting relations between persons and acts that arise from moral requirements not subject to waiver.

rights are redundant, comes to rely on their express authority even for liberties which ought to go without saying, and may no longer firmly believe in the liberties which, though they ought to go without saying, are not expressly spelt out. The door is then open to challenges, made and treated in a manner that misplaces the burden of proof.

Property is the outstanding example. In the United States, where specific written constitutional authority is held to be necessary for the protection of liberties (described as 'rights'), property rights are thought to be, albeit implicitly, affirmed by the 'due process' clause of the Constitution. Like every other text, this clause needs to be interpreted in application. As 'substantive' due process, it had for a time provided a ground for upholding the freedom of contract. In a different political tradition, the freedom of contract would be naturally presumed, and it is its infringement or limitation that would require a ground. Be that as it may, given the quirks and character of liberal doctrine, in the inter-war period the due process clause came to be re-interpreted and ceased effectively to protect the freedom of contract which became an easy target of Federal regulation. Such a shift could hardly have taken place if the liberty in question had not first been made dependent on the interpretation of a constitutional amendment—as if the burden of proof were on its defenders and not on its challengers.

Heedless of the burden of proof, Ronald Dworkin, a prominent liberal legal philosopher, states that it is a '*silly proposition* that true liberals must respect economic *as well as* intellectual liberty'.[1]

For this proposition to be 'silly'—that is, patently false, *a priori* groundless, requiring no rebuttal—it is necessary (though far from sufficient) that the two liberties in question should, as it were, be totally uncorrelated, disparate. They must have no common attribute, no shared feature that *could* possibly command recognition for both at the same time. Otherwise, liberals or others could have a reason to respect both, the reason arising on the same common ground. Such respect might be

---

[1] Dworkin, *op. cit.*, p. 264 (my italics). What Dworkin means by the somewhat indefinite term 'economic liberty' is presumably the freedom of contract, from which more specific 'economic' liberties can be deduced.

deserved or undeserved, but could not be plain silly, since it had a reason, though whether that reason was adequate or not might be a matter for argument.

However, if respecting one for the same reason that one respects the other is simply silly, and true liberals must respect intellectual but need not respect 'economic' liberty, there can be no common ground, no shared epistemological basis for their recognition.

Yet to suppose this is to ignore that, regardless of their substantive differences, both are 'freedoms', both involve Hohfeldian Y-relations, propositions which (like innocence) hold until proven false. Claim-rights do, but liberties do not require any particular evidence. The latter 'go without saying'. Even without calling respect for one freedom *because it is a freedom* like another, a 'silly proposition', to overlook the burden of proof is characteristic of the loose doctrine liberalism is well on the way to becoming. All it tells us for sure is that a right, liberty, power or immunity supported by the weightier *ad hoc* argument outweighs one supported by the less weighty, and which is which depends on who weighs them.

Part Two
STRICT LIBERALISM

4

FIRST PRINCIPLES

1. Finding Foundation Stones

IT IS A little-appreciated property of deductive reasoning that when we set up a system of axioms (propositions to be treated as agreed), we cannot as a rule predict all the consequences that may in the fullness of time be deduced from it.[1] The first principles set out in this chapter have been selected in the expectation that the exploration of their latent content will gradually unveil the theoretical outline of a political order which will be 'strictly liberal'.

It is intended to be *liberal*, a term I interpret minimally as presenting the least obstacles to men and women attaining, from available means, the ends they choose for themselves. A liberal order is not designed to augment, transform or redistribute the means, nor to promote the maximum attainment of stipulated ends, 'freedom' or any other desirable goal. It is intended to be *strict*, allowing little scope for discretionary interpretation; it is meant to give unambiguous guidance not only about what the state may or may not do to individuals without their consent, but more crucially also about what they can or cannot be supposed to have consented to. Liberal and strict, it is meant to take politics out of social co-existence as far as it will let itself be removed—a

---

[1] This point has been drawn to my attention by Gerard Radnitzky, the German philosopher. (*Cf.* W. W. Bartley, III, *Unfathomed Knowledge, Unmeasured Wealth*, La Salle, Ind.: Open Court, 1990, pp. 34-39.)

perhaps slightly cryptic objective whose meaning will become progressively clearer as we proceed.

The theory, if it were fully developed and exposed to the test of time, might not turn out quite as intended. At the very least, however, its foundations should be laid so as to make it as difficult as possible for the eventual structure to revert to loose liberalism. It should be hard for it to provide, albeit concealed between the lines, an implicit mandate for government to 'do good' whenever that is deemed possible. And it should not end up justifying the imposition of political choices on the ground that the resulting advantages to some people outweigh the drawbacks suffered by others.

Jobbing backwards from expected results to the first principles that should produce them is possible, and intellectually honest, to a restricted extent only. The principles chosen are not argued for. They must be self-evident; failing that, reasonable men should hold them indisputable; and failing that, too, they must at least make a strong appeal to the intuition. In addition, they must be non-redundant and sufficient, meaning that, taken together, they must adequately describe the basic features of a political system without making superfluous assertions.

Finally—and this is the most obvious but also a quite difficult requirement—they must not permit mutually contradictory deductions. To take the stock example, a system of political first principles which, once all its implications are worked out, is found to call *both* for the allocation of resources by the decentralised decisions of the resource owners themselves (to permit 'free-market efficiency'), *and* for their distribution by collective choice (to ensure 'social justice'), is internally self-contradictory. It is incapable of providing guidance; its indeterminacies and ambiguities must be overcome by discretion in judgement and in the use of political power. The results will seem good to some and bad to others, but they could have been reached more directly, without following the dubious and confused road signs of the hybrid political theory in question, and society would be no worse off if such a theory had never been propounded.

For all these reasons, the choice of principles, besides being only partially informed by the strict and internally consistent results we seek from them, is desperately restricted by the rarity of likely candidates. None of this excuses the shortcomings of the result, such as it is.

I am proposing to use six 'foundation stones'—three of them axioms of choice, three precepts of social co-existence:

(1) Individuals can, and only they can, choose (Individualism).

(2) Individuals can choose for themselves, for others or both (Politics).

(3) The point of choosing is to take the preferred alternative (Non-Domination).

(4) Promises shall be kept (Contract).

(5) First come, first served (Priority).

(6) All property is private (Exclusion).

Even if we cannot fully see the consequences of these principles and categorically state what they ultimately imply, in the balance of this chapter we will at least attempt to explore their plainest apparent meanings.

2. Three Basic Axioms on Choice

Contrary to widespread belief, the basic contentious issue of politics is not freedom, justice or equality. The latter are derivative problems. In the deepest sense, the issue is choice—*who* chooses *what* for *whom*—and what we hold true of choice determines the political theory we can or cannot accept. Liberals, I would affirm, must hold the following three statements true, and must not assent to political maxims, however familiar and innocuous, that would on closer inspection contradict them.

(1) *Individuals*[1] *Can, and* Only *They Can, Choose*

This will serve as the Individualism axiom. Its truth depends on restricting the meaning of the word 'choose'. This meaning is

---

[1] 'Individuals' is, somewhat imprecisely, intended to include 'families'. Although, taken literally, heads of families choose for themselves *and* for their dependents, I prefer to treat this case as if each member of the family chose for himself in happy unanimity and concord, rather than accepting the choice of the head of family. This falsifies reality, but allowing for conflicting preferences within families would introduce complications that are hardly relevant for the present purpose and that we are better off without.

narrower than the mere *taking* of one out of several mutually exclusive alternatives: for in the latter, wide sense herds of animals, groups of men, communities, all kinds of collections of individuals seeming to perform co-ordinated actions, can also 'choose'. The taking in the restricted sense of our axiom must be the outcome of consideration, however brief or cursory, of the reasons (benefits and costs, both taken broadly) speaking for and against each alternative. Individuals are held capable of considering the reasons for selecting one alternative rather than another, because of the universally accepted assumption that only they have minds. Groups, communities, nations do not consider, or do so only metaphorically.

A number of implications of the Individualism axiom springs to mind.

o First, it can be seen to assert that only individuals *can* make considered choices, not that they *do*. Both random picking and mindless, reflex choosing are consistent with the axiom. However, whether individuals make reasoned choices or not, ascribing to them a capacity to do so is making them responsible for their choices. The poverty of the alternatives they refuse does not absolve them from responsibility for the one that they do take; nobody else chose it for them, neither 'society' nor 'the system', for no such entity *can* choose.

o Secondly, they are not or only partly responsible for their choices if the reasons for and against are weighted by coercion (as defined on p. 14), and this must be the case whether the coercion is legitimate or not. Only the absence of coercion allows responsibility for one's actions to remain intact.

o Thirdly, the opposition of individual and collective (or 'social') choice is either a metaphor signifying nothing very definite, or collective choice, too, must be the outcome of individual choices in some, albeit indirect, fashion. Thus, the axiom by the same token prescribes methodological individualism as the only proper way of inquiring into the causes of social phenomena. To ask why, given the physical environment, a certain state of affairs prevails, is ultimately to ask why individuals chose it; the laws of historical development or the dynamics of class and race do not explain it.

o Fourthly, the axiom implies that uncoerced choice is

responsible but not that it is rational. It is open to a person to consider alternatives but he need not do so, and it is also possible for him adequately to consider every alternative, yet not to choose the one he finds best. The former is violating a weak, the latter a strong condition of rationality; but the axiom does not demand that any particular condition of rational choice be satisfied.

(2) *Individuals Can Choose for Themselves, for Others, or Both*

We shall call this the Politics axiom, and explain the axiom by justifying the name.

If a person could choose only for himself, only those alternatives would be open to him whose cost he could, so to speak, 'afford'. He could go to the cathedral, but he could not build one to go to. He could, if he were not too poor, buy a motor car, but he could not buy the roads to run it on even if he were very rich. Only three kinds of alternatives could possibly become available to him.

One is the unrequited kind: gifts of heaven or of his fellow men, of which his own offerings to heaven and his own gifts to his fellows were not direct, *quid pro quo* counterparts, expenditures destined to generate income. In certain primitive societies, unrequited gifts were a major part of a person's 'budget'. In the medieval and the modern world, two alternative kinds would predominate for the person who could choose only for himself. Either they were divisible into small enough units to fit into his 'budget' of time, energy, money; going to mass in the cathedral on Sunday would be such a small unit of the larger divisible good called 'religious observance'. A single motor car would likewise be a small enough unit of the larger entity 'the stock of motor cars'. A single individual could never choose the entity as a whole, but since it was divisible, he could choose bits of it, while if it took manoeuvres to divide it into accessible bits, in some cases someone could make it his business to do so. Thus, an entrepreneur could 'buy' a road and make its use divisible into small units—trips for cars from one toll booth to another.

The remaining alternatives are indivisible; the cathedral is a case in point. A cathedral might not lend itself to 'entrepreneurial' treatment at all (it would lose most of its point if only the paying faithful were admitted to it), and it is an open question whether it could get built at all if individuals could choose only for themselves and not for others; no minority could be forced by a majority to contribute to its cost and only voluntary, unanimous groups could undertake joint tasks of the cathedral-building kind.

In such a world, while it would be impossible for an individual to impose his choice on another, he would not run the risk of another doing it to him. In other words, each individual would be sovereign. Sovereignty, however, would be contingent on everybody bearing the opportunity cost of his choices. Bluntly, apart from windfalls, all would pay for what they got. Nobody could be made to pay for what somebody else got, nor could he make somebody else pay for what he got. In sum, the world would be one of free gifts and mutually acceptable exchanges only—rather like an unregulated, spontaneous market economy with consumer and producer sovereignty, and with charity possibly being encouraged by peer pressures but not made mandatory by coercion.

The moment choosing for others is admitted, everything changes. All physically feasible alternatives become available almost regardless of their scale. One individual can, in principle, choose cathedral-building for enough others for the necessary resources to be forthcoming. Needless to say, what goes for cathedrals goes for all other 'public goods' that are destined to be available to payers and non-payers alike.

This is not the juncture for going into the problem of public goods, though we shall have to pay some attention to them in Chapter 6. It may be, as some contend, that the whole category is a figment of the imagination of left-leaning economists and social critics, and that in reality all goods, from cathedrals, traffic lights and armies to knowledge and law, could be adequately supplied by allowing ordinary market incentives to operate. I lean (though not steeply) to the contrary view but shall not try to argue it here. For the present, it suffices to note that certain goods, even if they could be supplied by exchange mechanisms, are as a matter of fact provided by non-market, collective choices instead, and made freely available to all comers (like the protection of the law) or to all persons in a defined class (like state schools to school-age children). The goods so provided are *de facto* public, in the manner of the proverbial bird that waddled and quacked like a duck, and was one. Whether their intrinsic nature would have permitted goods that behave as public goods to behave as private ones instead, is not at issue.

At the end of this brief detour, it is perhaps clearer than it was before why we propose the possibility of choosing for others to be known as the Politics axiom. If the axiom did not hold, there could be no collective choices that were both *non-unanimous* and *binding*. Hence there could be no politics, only markets.

If the axiom holds, large-scale indivisible benefits can be chosen for many persons together, the cost of which can be shared out among many. Beneficiaries and contributors, however, need obviously not be the same, and none needs to pay exactly or even approximately for what he gets. Nothing prevents some from getting more than they pay for, others less. Many collective choices are undoubtedly made in order to produce precisely this result, not as a by-product of aiming at some other result, but as their central objective. The redistributive potential inherent in some being able to choose for others, and hence to generate gains and losses for distinct groups within a society, is probably the main underlying force that drives politics.

A liberal theory which did not allow for this possibility would be a case of Hamlet without the prince. It would be radically libertarian or, as some would put it, anarchist rather than liberal. Our purpose is not to defend libertarianism—it has enough arguments to look after itself—but to restate liberalism so that the place within it of the state and of politics should be more sharply defined. Hence the Politics axiom. Coming to terms with the consequences it conjures up—coercion, the 'tyranny of the majority', the rat race of interest groups forced (and failing) to keep one step ahead of one another—calls for powerful curbs. Failure to find curbs that work as intended is the Achilles' heel of the liberal order.

(3) *The Point of Choosing Is to Take the Preferred Alternative*

This will be referred to as the Non-Domination axiom. It signifies that choice is pointless if its result is to obtain a 'dominated' alternative, that is, one that is not at least as good as any other in a set of mutually exclusive options. Once again, this is not to affirm that people *never* choose dominated alternatives, only that it is a waste of their faculties if they do.

'Preferred' in this principle is used broadly as economists tend to use it, for whom it is the sum total of the diverse reasons why a person would rather have or do one thing than another. It is synonymous with the rank he assigns, for any number of possible reasons, to a given option within an hierarchical ordering of his available alternatives. In ordinary speech, 'preferring' is usually narrower: it is 'liking better', and tends to leave room for other reasons, such as moral duty or prudential interest, that a person may consider in deciding what he would rather do. The economist's 'preference' subsumes all operative reasons, and is more 'economical' to employ; but it must not prejudge the chooser's motivation. He may be a rigorously self-denying ascetic, a piggish hedonist, or most likely a bit of either depending on the occasion.

'Dominated' alternatives need elucidation in some detail. Selecting an option that is inferior to another one might have selected, may be no better than having a random machine doing the selection. The intrinsic purpose of conscious, considered choosing is precisely to obtain results superior to those offered by a random machine. It is to reduce the risk we would run if we relied on the latter—that is, of being dealt inferior, dominated alternatives. The faculty to choose (itself a compound of other, more basic human faculties, including perception, evaluation, anticipation, decision, and perhaps several others), though its design might not be perfect, is the best means human beings have for getting what they would rather have. By and large, it enables its own intrinsic purpose to be fulfilled, and there is no other conceivable mechanism for doing it.

While not using this faculty is a *waste*, frustrating it is *wrong*. It is wrong in the fairly plain sense that making a person take a dominated alternative that he can be presumed not to have taken otherwise, is to injure him. The tort he suffers is twofold: it resides both in the damage to his interests and in the violation of his liberty to choose.

There is, however, a less plain, more abstract but no less important sense in which frustrating the faculty to choose is wrong. This is the sense in which frustrating any human faculty without good cause is wrong. Christians would say that it is wrong in that it goes against God's design of man. In secular ethics, one would invoke, along much the same lines, the integrity of the person as he is, an integrity that is mutilated when, in an attempt to change his aspirations, perhaps to make him more 'social', his faculties are prevented from fulfilling their intended purpose.[1] This is a separate injury, different from the one he suffers when he is made to take a lesser in place of a greater good.

The Non-Domination axiom, if agreed to be a self-evident principle, represents an implicit bar to paternalism. Why, however, should we bar paternalism?—why is it wrong, if it is true, as it no doubt is, that some people are apt to make themselves quite miserable if left to make their own choices? Strict liberalism takes no explicit position about people who are unable to choose because they manifestly lack some of the basic faculties that go to make up the faculty of choosing. It gives no mandatory guidance about drunkards, drug addicts, or the insane. For those manifestly able to choose, however, it excludes paternalism. Its interdiction obviously cannot be defended on any direct consequentialist ground. *Liberalism*, however, *is not about making people better off* in any immediate and pragmatic way. It is about the organising principles of a society *where people are most likely to learn to make themselves better off*. If it has a consequentialist justification, it is this longer-term and indirect one. Of course it has, in addition, a non-consequentialist defence which, however, need not be invoked on the score of paternalism.

Paternalism, as it was shown in Chapter 2, stands condemned anyway by loose liberalism's Harm Principle, but the latter, for

---

[1] Arguing from the intrinsic purpose of a faculty formally resembles arguing from the 'internal goal of an activity'. Bernard Williams is said to be doing the latter when he claims that the internal goal of medical care is to heal the sick, hence it would be wrong to dispense it only to the sick who can pay for it. (*Cf.* B. Williams, 'The Idea of Equality', in P. Laslett and W. G. Runciman (eds.), *Philosophy, Politics and Society*, 2nd series, Oxford: Basil Blackwell, 1962.) Nozick attacks this line of thought on the ground that an activity need not be characterised by one, or indeed any, internal goal. Barbering serves not or not only the barbering need of the bearded, but also or perhaps only the 'needs' of the barber that make him exercise his trade. (*Cf.* R. Nozick, *op. cit.* pp. 233-34.) Nozick's reasoning seems decisive as regards 'activities', but it cannot be extrapolated to 'faculties'. The *activity* of fishing has either no internal goal, or it is to catch fish, or to pass the time agreeably. By contrast, the *faculty* of sight has seeing as its intrinsic purpose; if we lived in absolute darkness, it would become absolutely pointless (and would duly wither away).

all its attractiveness, is less effective in protecting individual choice in all the other cases, where paternalism is not an issue. It can be turned until it sounds as if it called for imposing worse choices on some for the greater good of others. Non-Domination, however, has a force (and to fall in with the ballistic metaphor of Ronald Dworkin, a 'range' as well) for hitting bigger targets than paternalism with greater precision. For it condemns, not merely that A should choose in B's place for B's own good. It condemns also, and with equal severity, the imposition of dominated options for whatever other reason, including re-distributive aims as well as holistic conceptions of goals and goods.[1] What the second axiom recognises as a *de facto* possibility and an obvious menace, namely politics, the third axiom appears to brand as an offence against reason, against the use of natural faculties as they are made to be used.

Lest it be thought that there *can* be no politics without partly defeating the purpose, the central point of individual choice, we must anticipate a turning we shall come to further down the road. The third axiom leaves a gap, to be explored at that turning. If there is a category of alternatives that individuals would rather have than any other mutually exclusive ones, but cannot have *unless they were chosen by others* as well, politics as collective choice confined to these alternatives may be consistent with the Non-Domination principle. What these alternatives might be, and how one tells whether they really exist, are questions that do not seem to have plain and sure answers. The principal and (as I believe) cleansing effect of strict liberalism's third principle is precisely to direct the searchlight of doubting, critical scrutiny on to these very special alternatives.

---

[1] Why should holistic conceptions of the good not be imposed, if they cannot be attained without imposition? It has been contended that certain features of social life, such as equality or fairness, are good in themselves, and 'their value does not rest on their being good things *for particular individuals*'. (T. M. Scanlon, 'Rights, Goods and Fairness', in J. Waldron (ed.), *Theories of Rights*, Oxford: OUP, 1984, p. 143 (my italics).) If there are such goods, justice is one of them. If its value does not depend on its being good for particular persons (or perhaps all of them), we must approve the principle of *fiat justitia pereat mundus*—'may the whole world perish, but let there be justice'. But after all potential beneficiaries of justice have perished, how would justice prevail? One gets into awkward self-contradictions by postulating goods that bring no benefits, and benefits that have no beneficiaries.

3. Three Basic Principles of Social Co-existence

Choice is exercised within some framework of conventions and rights, serving in some cases to attenuate and in others to adjudicate conflicts among alternatives various persons would choose. This framework rests on the recognition, by moral intuition, of basic precepts of social co-existence. Three of these, in particular, seem conducive to the voluntariness and spontaneity of the framework. They contribute to its consistency with the choice axioms, in particular with Non-Domination.

(4) *Promises Shall Be Kept*

This principle is the moral basis, not only of unilateral commitments, but of the institution of contract, a cornerstone of all social co-existence. In what follows, it will be called the Contract principle.

Some contracts, to wit those for simultaneous exchanges, are self-enforcing or tend to be so. Others, however, contain in their time-and-performance structure an incentive to default. They require enforcement for the commitment of one party to be credible to the other. It is not suggested that the practice of reciprocal commitment would become impossible if *pacta sunt servanda* were not accepted as an undisputed moral norm. Quite conceivably though not certainly, both promise and contract might subsist on the sole strength of some collectively maintained enforcing mechanism devoid of the support of a widely shared belief in the wrongness of breach of promise. The question of its survival (and of the survival of the enforcing mechanism itself) under such conditions is moot. It is a particular case of the more general question of the survival of norm and law, when conformity to it is enforced by a coercive authority but is not cemented by approval and respect. No possible answer stands out as especially plausible, and the question is probably destined to remain wide open. It is clear, however, that even if law without respect for law, contract without belief in the morally binding force of the given word and in the shamefulness of default, were possible and viable, their survival would presuppose heavily coercive arrangements ultimately incompatible with a liberal order.

On the other hand, if a preponderant part of society considers that keeping promises is a moral duty, its breach and hence default on contracts will provoke disapproval and adverse reactions from a wider circle than the victim and his natural allies. Social sanctions represent the beginnings of enforcement by impartial third parties—perhaps imperfect, but enforcement all the same even in the complete absence of any formal apparatus relying on sovereign power. The promisee who falls victim to default enjoys the favourable disposition of neutral bystanders and has some chance of enlisting their help. The defaulting promisor has some reason to fear their hostility, their reluctance to have dealings with him in the future, and eventually their pressure to secure redress for the victim. These standard social reactions are familiar and have an illustrious past going back to antiquity and beyond.[1]

Their potential force in a modern society is, for obvious reasons, ill appreciated. It is overlaid by the formal judicial superstructure that fully-fledged states provide as a public good, and that leaves little need and even less scope for the spontaneous provision of enforcement. It is, however, relevant to liberal theory to retain the fact that making enforcement a public rather than a private concern is by no means the sole way of ensuring that contracts are credible and can be relied on.[2] The belief, ceaselessly advanced as if it were an established truth, that contracts are simply not enforceable without the political authority assuming the task, and that consequently 'the state is prior to the market', with the market being the fragile creature of an institutional framework built and upheld by the sovereign

---

[1] Contempt for the man who will not (or even *cannot*) keep his word, triggering sanctions, is a marked feature of most primitive societies. Attitudes become more forgiving, and social sanctions fade away, as enforcement shifts from spontaneous processes to the formal machinery of the state. A valid contract is no longer an agreement the parties have shaken hands on; it becomes instead what lawyers think will stand up in court.

[2] Interesting evidence to this effect is that in classical Roman legal practice, in civil actions only the judgement was a matter for the court, its enforcement being the private concern of the plaintiff. Even for adjudication, the monopoly of state courts as we know it, is but a special case: there is a multitude of examples in history of private adjudication by trusted peers and semi-professional arbitrators having knowledge of the subject at issue. Nor is there much reason to assume that these private arrangements were not as fair and expeditious as the later state monopoly—though a comparative assessment could of course never be incontestable.

government, is a wholly arbitrary one. It is unsupported by theory and falsified by history. Medieval mercantile law, which was totally 'stateless',[1] and was enforced essentially by peer pressure, demonstrates empirically that there is no intrinsic necessity nor inherently greater efficiency in enforcement by the state. The incentive to default, built into the very nature of certain (partly forward or 'executory') contracts, by no means implies that the institution of contract presupposes the state. The rôle of the latter follows, not from the nature of contracts, but from the richly lucrative revenue potential offered by a monopoly of contract enforcement, which drove royal courts to secure it for themselves.

However, it is important not to confuse two independent claims about promises. One is that the possibility of making credible commitments is such a priceless advance in economic relations, so immense a help in solving otherwise perhaps insoluble conflicts between individuals who would all be better off co-operating but need the assurance of reciprocity to do so, that all potential contracting parties will be actively interested in shoring up the credibility of commitments.

One way or another, they will see to it that contracts are as a rule enforced, and will be prepared to face trouble, strife, costs to that end. Whether they do it only or mainly for their own contracts, or for those of anybody else on a mutual aid basis, individually or in organisations, case-by-case or as standard practice, is from this 'functional' point of view a secondary question. This claim, then, deduces the willingness of any random individual to help enforce contracts and incur costs to do it, from a cold calculus of the benefits he (and his kin and descendants) can expect from the institution.

Some legal and economic theories indeed ascribe the social recognition of the duty to honour contracts, and its socially generated sanctions, to the economic *value to society* of credible reliance. These theories are somewhat problematical, for reliance is a public good to the extent that defaulters and non-enforcers, who do not contribute to upholding the institution of contract,

---

[1] *Cf.* L. E. Trakman, *The Law Merchant: The Evolution of Commercial Law*, Littleton, Col.: Fred B. Rothman & Co., 1983, and B. L. Benson, 'The Spontaneous Evolution of Commercial Law', *Southern Economic Journal*, Vol. 55, 1989.

benefit from it just as much as those who do. Consequently, the cost-benefit calculus to a given individual is not as unambiguously in favour of incurring costs to protect contracts, as these theories seem to assume. The balance of benefit may in fact induce an individual to contribute, but hardly because there is an aggregate, *social* benefit, however large, for all individuals taken together.

The other, moral claim on our duty does not directly arise from any benefit we may expect (though there is an indirect connection). It is derived instead from the Kantian notion of the intrinsic purpose of a faculty—a notion already invoked above with regard to the Non-Domination axiom. The purpose of speaking is to convey information content to another; lying may well serve the *ad hoc* purpose of the liar, but if all lied, the purpose of speaking would be defeated, for no one would put any value on what was being conveyed. Similarly, the purpose of promising is to make one's commitment to a course of action reliable for another; breaking the promise may suit the defaulter, but if all broke theirs, promising would become wholly pointless. (The Kantian test of rationally moral conduct is not whether an individual might rationally wish to lie, but whether he could rationally wish that others should lie, i.e. that his desired conduct should be 'universalisable'.) However, it is wrong that a human faculty designed to serve a useful purpose should become pointless, lose its purpose. Therefore all have the duty to keep promises, regardless of whether they personally expect to benefit from the usefulness of the practice of promising.

Moreover, if breaking one's promise is a wrong independently of any harm done to the promisee, it is wrong whether or not the promise was contingent on a *quid pro quo*. An unrequited promise, then, is morally as worthy of enforcement as one made against 'value received'. Determining the remedy for breach of an unrequited promise that caused no damage to the promisee may be controversial. It remains the case, however, that if one strong reason why we must honour contracts is that we must keep promises—a reason 'loose-liberal' jurisprudence does not think is strong at all—contracts must be honoured and enforced regardless of whether they are 'one-sided'. The inadequacy of the agreed consideration a party is to get in exchange for his performance, is no excuse for failing to perform as promised. In this respect, both classical Roman law and the common law adopt the uncompromising 'formalist' practice of refusing to judge the validity of a contract by the equitableness of the consideration.[1] They take this position in their wisdom; strict liberalism takes it because it is implicit in its system of first principles.

Both the benefit-oriented and the duty-oriented explanation of the respect in which promises ought to be, or are, held, are consistent with the Contract principle. Both help to underpin it. Both go some way towards showing why the duty to honour contracts appears as intuitively obvious, self-evident to most of us (at least as long as we remain uncontaminated by philosophical or legal sophistication). They mutually re-inforce each other in providing grounds why people will usually try to keep their promises and discharge their obligations even when their palpable interest would dictate otherwise, and why they have since earliest times been prepared to go to trouble and expense to sanction (penalise) breaches.

(5) *First Come, First Served*

The rôle of this, the Priority principle, is to help regulate the exercise of 'liberties' in a crowded social environment. Liberties, as we have found in the logical analysis of rights (see Box, above, pp. 48-49), are in principle unlimited unless proof of a limitation is shown in the form of another's right that the exercise of the liberty would infringe. There are, however, contexts when no right appears to limit a liberty, none can be shown, yet its exercise conflicts with the exercise of a liberty by others. It may be the same liberty, for example, two people trying to sing different solo arias, or a different liberty, for example, one singing the aria and the other trying to sleep in the same room.

If 'first come, first served' seems self-evident or, failing that, reasonable enough to most people, 'crowded' liberties shall be exercised in succession, and need not 'bump' into each other. It is to suggest this sequential solution that I propose to name it the Priority principle.

Anyone who has admired, in a Moscow railway station, the

---

[1] It should be noted that the contrary position is taken in civil law systems: *cf.* B. Nicholas, *An Introduction to Roman Law*, Oxford: OUP, 1975, p. 175.

holder of a Writers' Union pass going to the head of a queue of several hundred people waiting to buy tickets; or black leather-clad motor-cycle police with their sirens screaming, parting Paris traffic in front of some official's car, will understand the moral basis of priorities. In the former case, Culture gets priority, in the latter, Public Service.

'First come, first served' has no such moral basis. It is, to use a fashionable term, 'morally arbitrary', for there is no evident moral ground for giving first to the one who came first. Its distance from any moral ground, rather than reliance on a particular moral ground, provides the principle's brute strength.

Its scope is wider than it seems. Fairly obviously, it underlies many conventions about access to scarce space and time. Its various manifestations: bookings, the order books of manu-facturers, the appointment diaries of doctors, parking space, waiting lists for housing or hospital beds, all represent easy-to-adopt, easy-to-administer solutions to problems of excess demand for resources that are either priced too cheaply or are altogether un-priced. It comes into its own when the price mechanism does not, or cannot conveniently be asked to, reconcile otherwise incompatible claims. It is the basis of the convention of queuing, and the reason why most people regard queuing as irksome but equitable (short only of requiring those unable to wait and in grave need, to take their turn). It is, finally, the root principle that regulates the distribution of prizes in free competitions of all kinds in business, sport or the arts, according to the order of arrival at some finishing line.

In all these conventions, liberties are exercised that would need no curb in an uncrowded setting, but that it is desirable for civilised co-existence to prevent from 'bumping' into each other when their setting is crowded. This is to a large extent achieved by acceptance of 'first come, first served'.

Like any first principle, this one, too, has far-reaching implications. We cannot hope promptly to discover more than a few. One that is readily apparent bears on the current urge to administer 'social justice' to distributions of goods, privileges, advantages that are considered to be 'morally arbitrary'. The Priority principle imposes one particular order on how one person's liberty is to rank relative to another's, and on who shall accede to something scarce and valuable to which no one has better title than anyone else but which only some can have. This order of priority is the order of arrival in a designated position, or of the making of the relevant claim. It is morally arbitrary if by 'moral' we mean something like 'justified by deserts'.

There is no merit in coming first nor in claiming first, nor any other reason, such as unequal effort, unequal contribution, unequal pain or abstinence, that would provide any unequal distribution with a moral basis. Yet the principle does not strike us as unjust; on the contrary, it is widely held to be equitable, almost certainly because it is felt to be impartial as a distributor of inequality. This suggests that 'moral arbitrariness' is far from being the damning indictment that it is made out to be by theorists of distributive justice.

A 'morally arbitrary' distribution cannot validly be objected to in the absence of rights to a 'non-arbitrary' one. On the other hand, if rights are to be created to some kind of passage from a morally arbitrary to a morally based distribution, on what grounds are such rights to be assigned? If 'culture' is a good ground in Moscow, and 'public service' in Paris, many other rival grounds can be found without going very far from home. Their relative merits and priorities must somehow be decided. This cannot be conclusively done without having them churned out by the political process. The result will not be morally arbitrary, but on the contrary morally biased, and quite likely less acceptable to the moral intuitions of all whose favourite moral principles or important interests failed to prevail.

To make certain that the difference between the arbitrariness of drawing lots and the bias of ranking one moral basis above another is clearly understood, take the morally arbitrary case of two passers-by who both notice a £10 note on the ground a little way off.[1] Neither has a right to it, and neither has a duty to hang back and let the other get it. Whichever of the two picks it up first (perhaps scrambling and stooping at some cost to his dignity, or perhaps simply because he was quicker to spot it and quicker off the mark) will be regarded as justified in not sharing it with the other. This is no doubt morally arbitrary, but so would sharing it be, unless a moral principle regulating such cases were to be

---

[1] The example is Herbert Hart's in his classic paper 'Are There Any Natural Rights?', *Philosophical Review*, Vol. 64, 1955.

introduced and accepted. Regulating it by 'first come, first served' is random; re-regulating it necessarily involves a bias relative to randomness, partiality to one or another moral distributive principle relative to the impartiality of a mechanical distributive device that does not seek to determine moral deserts.

'First come, first served', if agreed, validates *finders' keepers'*. If there is no pre-existing right to the contrary, and none can be created on plausible grounds, possession gives rise to presumption of title to property. First possession is the natural consequence of first finding and claiming. Nothing more complicated than this is needed to provide the solution of the old problem of legitimate original acquisition, which has tormented generations of social theorists. For many (though by no means all of them), voluntary, agreed transfer of a property right from one holder to another was itself valid (or, at its scholastic worst, it was valid if ceded at a 'just price'); but how was the very first holder's right justified to begin with, since he did not acquire it from another holder of valid title?

Before Locke, it was held that since disputing the first occupant's title (to land) would have led to endless strife over who 'really' ought to have it, men have little by little come to accept it as a justified, natural right, on a par with property rights validly transferred by previous title-holders. Locke thought that he both needed and could provide a morally firmer, deeper defence for the genesis of a property right, by marrying first occupancy with two famous provisos. The first occupant had to 'mix his labour' with the land to make it his, and 'enough and as good' had to be left over for later-comers for the first occupant's claim to title to be good.

The latter proviso can be dismissed as one that it is impossible to fulfil except in fanciful conditions of abundance, where property rights are irrelevant in any case, so that it does not matter how valid they are. If there is a state of abundance, but it looks *temporary*, as at the outset of a land rush on the frontier of settlement, the first occupant is bound to assume that before the land rush is anywhere near over, there will not be enough and as good land left for others, and therefore his first occupancy does not justify title; while in *permanent* abundance the problem simply does not arise.

The 'mixing his labour' proviso has the congenital

weaknesses[1] of all labour theories of justified acquisition and value. Entertaining as it may be to dissect them, for the present it suffices to note the obvious, namely that making the justified origin of property dependent *both* on 'finders' keepers' *and* on there being enough left for others *and* on one's labour, weakens rather than strengthens the moral status of any given distribution of property, for any distribution is likely to violate one or two of these several conditions. It creates a vacuum for other, 'juster' theories of distribution to fill.

The manifold political consequences of the rise of such theories are familiar. Social reformers, unsurprisingly, may consider them good 'on balance'. They are certainly not strictly liberal, in that they call for continuous and discretionary re-allocation of property rights among people. By virtue of the Priority principle, strict liberalism refrains from questioning the *initial* allocation. To those who rightly point out that this is leaving starting positions to chance, and who go on to claim, more contestably, that chance is even less just than political discretion, one can only answer that this is not a matter to which it is proper to apply the category of justice. Matters to which it *is* proper to apply it have to do with the consequences of rights, and it is gratuitous (or an appeal to peculiar metaphysics) to assert that there are rights to property prior to its initial distribution—rights to which effect must be given in order for the distribution to be just.

(6) *All Property Is Private*

This is best called the Exclusion principle, for it permits an individual in whom a property right is vested, to exclude others

---

[1] Locke first posits that if man owns himself, he owns his labour. (This, however, does not in itself permit the conclusion that he owns the fruit of his labour, too, if there is some doubt whether such fruit is the product of his labour *alone*.) He then explains that if man takes something as nature left it and 'mixes his labour with it', he joined to that thing 'something that is his own, and thereby makes it his property'. (J. Locke, *Of Civil Government* (1690), Second Treatise, London: J. M. Dent, 1924, p. 26 (my italics).) Surely, however, the 'thereby' is a *non-sequitur*. If the thing was not his to begin with, it is not his now, whatever he added to it. To 'mix' his labour with it, without independently making sure that he will have title to the entire new mixture, seems rash, to put it no higher.

both from the decisions inherent in the right,[1] and from their consequences. Neither is 'ours', neither is *shared* according to 'ought-claims', needs or votes. The principle discourages beliefs that the property-owner is under some obligation to non-owners, and must let them participate in decisions regarding his property or the benefits it yields. If there are such obligations, the burden is on the claimants to prove it.

Exclusion is not self-evident; it is perhaps not evident at all at first sight as a generally valid principle, for in everyday language we do talk of 'common property' that does not have identifiable individual owners (natural or legal persons) whose quantified rights would exclude those of anyone else. Collective ownership would imply that some or all rights pertaining to the use and disposal of an asset are held jointly by a group of persons and are unapportioned among its members. Admission to the group may be controlled or free; those inside the group have claims to the asset without owning a definite, quantified share in it; all those outside the group are excluded. (Common property from which *nobody* is excluded is, of course, a contradiction in terms. Something is either property, or freely accessible to all and entailing no rights all comers could not benefit from.)

Why, then, do we seek to reserve the term 'property' to individual and deny it to collective ownership?—and why do we insist that there is, properly speaking, no such thing as 'our' property, nor does property have 'social obligations'?

The fundamental reason is that, after duly weighing all the doubts that legal theorists cast on the exact significance of ownership, there is one irreducible, residual element that constitutes ownership if nothing else does: it is the right to decide about the use and disposal of the rights[2] pertaining to the asset owned, namely about the rights of use, usufruct and alienation. However, for a theory that does not recognise collective minds, collective owners as such are not able to decide. Only individuals can, and the ones (whether singly or in coalitions, majorities) who do, decide for all in the collectivity. Collective choice on behalf of

---

[1] It should be recalled that a property right is a compound of a 'right' in the strict sense, and of a 'liberty'. Both reserve certain decisions to their holder.

[2] Ownership, then, is a 'meta-right' or 'super-right' exercised over property rights. (*Cf.* Ch. 5, 4 (c) below, pp. 98-103.)

any group is 'political' choice except in the borderline case of unanimity, and so, for the same reason, is collective ownership.[1] Still for the same reason, collective ownership defeats the very purpose of property, which is to vest in individuals the sovereignty over the employment of scarce resources. Sovereignty over certain types of decisions may be delegated revocably, or transferred for good, but it cannot be shared,[2] and this is why there is no true property that, after cancelling out agents, delegates and intermediaries, is not mine, yours, his or hers.

Where does this leave commonalty, 'common pool ownership', the village green, the worker commune, municipal or state property?—not to forget the undefinable category 'social property', of which we know only what it is not? It leaves them all outside property in the strict sense. They do not answer to the intrinsic purpose of the institution; in fact, they are *designed* to defeat, overcome or circumvent its purpose. They avoid the qualifying condition, essential for property fo fulfil its moral and instrumental functions, that responsibility for decisions (even delegated ones) about the use and transfer of property rights should be borne by the same person who bears the costs and reaps the benefits of the decisions. Under collective ownership, no part of this triple identity of decision-maker, cost-bearer and beneficiary need or indeed *can* normally be satisfied.

This is both a moral defect, and a denial of the rôle property rights are meant to play in bringing about efficient resource allocation. These are two independent indictments. Either of the

---

[1] The Non-Domination principle implies that since collective choice may select dominated alternatives that some in the collectivity do not prefer (and conceivably none prefers), it frustrates the intrinsic purpose of choice. This alone establishes a presumption against collective ownership, too, so that the Exclusion principle may have no work left to do. However, the 'point' of property is wider than the 'point' of choosing. Exclusion is not entailed in Non-Domination and is not made redundant by it. Property is meant to shape and allocate incentives, focusing in individuals the benefits and costs that would otherwise be diluted over vague groups. Its *moral purpose* (the identification of responsibility) and its *instrumental function* (the 'internalising' of what would otherwise be 'external') are more complex than those of choice.

[2] 'Shared sovereignty' is another contradiction in terms, much like 'common property'. If a set of decision-makers 'shares' sovereignty over certain alternatives, its members either agree unanimously, or part of the set decides for the rest and is sovereign *over it*, rather than sharing sovereignty *with it*.

two may be dismissed without refuting the other. Both, however, are bound up with property's 'point', which presupposes that it is private, not public and political.

This is not, in itself, a plea for abolishing the village common, unapportioned fishing grounds or nationalised industry. The former tend to give rise to overgrazing and overfishing,[1] the latter are beset by notorious agency problems. Each leaves unpunished the irresponsible use of resources, when it does not positively reward it. However, it is perfectly possible for these defects to be outweighed, in some eyes, by countervailing merits. Such countervailing merits form part of a value-hierarchy and of a political order that contradicts strict liberalism. Understanding this is not, however, a reason to deny or dispute them.

Lest there be misunderstandings, individual ownership does not mean that rights over a given asset *must* be assigned to a given individual. A vast property, indivisible like a railway or a ship, or divisible but undivided like the far-flung facilities of a large corporation, may be owned by many individuals of modest means in severalty, if the rights to the property are themselves divisible. The joint-stock company, of course, is the archetypal form of individual ownership in severalty. Ownership of a single asset by a single individual can be regarded as a special, limiting case of it.

Before passing on, it might be helpful to deal with another misconception. Because of the pleasing, intellectually undemanding nature of the 'stages-of-history' and 'laws-of-development' type of theories, the idea that common pool ownership belongs to one stage, private property to another, has taken a strong hold. Many people came to believe, for instance, that primitive communism, peasant property, feudal serfdom and capitalist ownership formed a necessary sequence, to be followed, if the laws of development are duly observed, by 'social ownership'. Whether the exact sequence, let alone its continuation into the future, is got right or not, the underlying idea is that forms of ownership adapt to historical contingencies. This is almost certainly a groundless belief. The practices of private

---

[1] For the conditions that may enable this tendency to be countered, *cf.* E. Ostrom, *Governing the Commons*, Cambridge: Cambridge University Press, 1990.

property are as old as the withdrawal of families into separate households and that, in turn, is nearly as old as *homo sapiens*. Private property in producers' goods, including such large undivided objects as longboats and hunting grounds, was widely adopted by many hunter-gatherer peoples. Down to our day, both private and collective property subsist, their proportionate share undergoing ups and downs, often for no very clear cause. It is probable that less private property is a handicap to development, more is an aid. But there is no trace of a causal relation the other way round, with stages of development dictating the system of property rights appropriate to them.

The causes and motivational springs of property are rooted in alternative logical relations between persons, acts and things. These relations are abstract, and their interactions, producing incentives and resistances, do not depend on time and place. One must be careful in sorting out what this means. It does not mean that one system of property rights is as suitable and intrinsically as worthy of respect and protection as another, and it is up to 'society' to choose the one it will protect. This was basically the original utilitarian position,[1] and it is one that loose liberalism, too, is leaning towards:[2] collective choice is free to set such limits to individual choice in matters of property as it sees fit, for good reasons, the plainest one being that individuals are unable to protect their property from each other, and can enjoy only the rights that 'society' is willing collectively to enforce.

It cannot be said often enough that this view is wrong.

o First, it grossly overstates the need for an organised government being the 'monopolist of legitimate coercion' as a protector of property. History has provided sufficient evidence that spontaneous, decentralised arrangements are capable of protecting property about as well as it ever *is* protected; that

---

[1] *Cf.* Alan Ryan's admirable summary of it, which could in fact be a summary of much contemporary discourse, too:

'Property rights are not natural liberties but social privileges, and we *have* only those property rights which the law gives us. The further question of what rights the law *should* give us is, in Mill's view, one to be settled on grounds of general utility, even if general utility can contain a large element of liberty promotion.'

(A. Ryan, *Property and Political Theory*, Oxford: Blackwells, 1984, p. 144.)

[2] For example, J. Rawls, *op. cit.*, pp. 274-84.

they do not and cannot in the presence of the state is a tautology entailed in the latter's monopoly of coercion, and like other tautologies, it proves nothing.

o Secondly, it overestimates the extent to which 'society' can tinker with, shape, modulate, limit or re-assign property rights without incurring costly consequences it is then unwilling to accept. Recent inglorious retreats from 'social property' in a number of countries illustrate this dilemma.

o Thirdly, it is wrong, too, because it misconstrues the moral significance of private property as a strong and straightforward relation between persons, acts and valuable resources. This relation, amounting to the threefold identity of the person responsible for choices, the one bearing their costs and the one benefiting from them, is severed when property is collectively owned. The breach violates the requirement that people must be fully responsible for the consequences of their choices. That we cannot always ensure that this should be so is no good reason for violating the requirement even if we could. Hence whether 'society' chooses private or collective property or some wishful attempt at finding a half-way house between them, is not something it should decide on independent grounds, indifferent to what property is designed to achieve—in brief, ignoring its 'point'.

It happens that the moral significance of property has a (not quite fortuitous) by-product. When the moral requirement inherent in individual ownership is satisfied, certain necessary conditions of efficient resource allocation are by the same token also fulfilled: it pays the allocator to allocate optimally, it hurts him not to. The equality of all discounted future marginal revenues and marginal costs under perfect competition may be an impossibly elusive target, if only because it exists only by anticipation, in people's heads. Yet for private property, there are at least stronger incentives to seek such equality than any other objective. Under collective ownership, other targets are rationally preferable for the persons responsible for target-selection.

This ought to weigh heavily with those who ask of a political system that it should promote economic efficiency. It weighs rather less in strict liberal theory, since the latter is only indirectly concerned with economic performance, leaving it to individual choices. Nevertheless, it is a comforting thought that what meets the moral requirements of strict liberalism turns out to be a necessary condition of economic efficiency, too.

5

CONVENTION
AND CONTRACT

ALL CHOICE is restricted to available sets of mutually exclusive options: when I go for a walk, I cannot sit by the fire, and what I spend I cannot save. Availability is enclosed within two ring fences: it is a matter both of physical feasibility and of the chooser's resource endowments, his 'budget' of time, money, knowledge and strength of will. The limits of availability are inherent in the very concept of choice and need to be stated only for the sake of formal completeness. However, it would be absurd to speak of choosing the unattainable. On the other hand, human co-existence (and for that matter the co-existence of living beings in general) entails that not all available choices are admissible. Civilisation limits the freedom of choice so as to reduce its destructive potential. Unlike availability, admissibility is not inherent in the idea of choice. It is a product of social interaction. It is probably safe to say that the manner of setting limits to choice—the trade-off between free choice and risk of harm—is, through various feedbacks, a powerful influence on the evolution of a civilisation. A police state, a society of yeomen and burghers, or one of salaried public employees—each has its own manner of circumscribing choice, and each continues to be shaped by the manner it has adopted.

Mainstream social theory tends to reason as if the limits of admissibility were, as a matter of necessity, set by the law which defines crimes, torts, liabilities and rights, and also provides the sanctions meant to deter inadmissible choices. But this is by no means a necessary truth if by 'law' we must mean law—and predominantly statute law—emanating from a sovereign authority, eliciting 'society's' collective wishes in legislation, and equipped with the power to enforce it. The law-making, rights-creating and -enforcing state is an historically contingent institution, not a logical necessity. It is always worthwhile to inquire into the causes and reasons for its persistence. But it is a lame and tame political theory that cannot rise above it and see it as merely one of several possible cases. In the present chapter, we shall attempt to think of social organisation in a very general manner, without pre-empting an explicit rôle for the state. Instead of assuming it, we shall perhaps learn more by letting it, so to speak, intrude into the analysis (as it will do with some force in Chapter 6) and letting its strictly liberal rôle define itself through the actual workings of liberalism's fundamental principles.

Without prejudging, therefore, the existence and source of state law, I will consider the drawing of the boundaries of admissible choices by spontaneously arising *conventions* and *rights* created by agreement. I will be asking where they might be expected to come from, whether they can be relied on, and whether they can possibly conform to liberal first principles.

1. Conventions As Tacit Contracts

A convention is best understood as an informally concluded tacit contract loosely binding a large number of people. The performance it aims at is, at its simplest, conformity of the parties to a common norm. It is loose because it does not stipulate total conformity. It demands it only in a probabilistic sense, so that the tacit contract is honoured, and the convention both fulfils its purpose and survives, if some proportion of the parties at any one moment conforms to the norm. Only in the case of very sensitive conventions—perhaps only in the case of the convention against matricide or high treason—must it be understood to require absolute compliance.

Obviously, the required degree of conformity must depend on the vulnerability to non-compliance both of the convention's utility and of its survival. The entire utility of the convention to drive on the left is in jeopardy if one motorist in a hundred drives on the right instead, whereas the utility of drinking one's soup without slurping will at worst fall in proportion to the number who slurp; even if many do, the non-slurping convention remains an agreeable amenity thanks to the virtuous minority who do not slurp. On the other hand, the convention to queue will not survive if many keep jumping the queue, while that against theft tends to survive even a local epidemic of thieving.

A convention is only metaphorically a contract because it involves no explicit nor even implicit undertakings to perform. Nor do the parties really intend to enter into reciprocal commitments. They nonetheless find themselves in a relation to one another where each can attach a significant probability to the others conforming to the spontaneously emerging norm. The metaphor of a contract is seductive despite the incongruities between it and the convention, because both are quintessentially voluntary, and both represent what, in technical language, amount to Pareto-improvements. The term refers to a change, for instance a new kind of social arrangement, that some of those affected by it would welcome and none would oppose if they were offered the chance. Such 'unanimity with abstentions' means that the change is an improvement *because* it is distributed in such a manner that at least some are better off and none worse off; the improvement is indisputable even in the most severely agnostic, positivist frame of reference, because for no one is it a worsening. (A Pareto-optimal, or 'efficient', arrangement, in turn, is one incapable of Pareto-improvement, reached when all possible Pareto-improvements have already been made. It is a state of affairs that no one can change to his advantage without another opposing the change.)

Both the contract and the convention produce a benefit available for sharing among the parties. In the case of the contract, the potential benefit is usually assumed to be sufficient incentive for the parties to seek out each other and reach a bargain on the terms that distribute the joint benefit between them. The information, search and bargaining costs, and for good measure the 'enforcement costs' as well, are subsumed under the somewhat question-begging term of transactions costs. These are imputed costs whose magnitude cannot as a rule be independently ascertained, but only inferred from the actions of the parties involved: if a contract is in fact concluded, the potential benefit (the gains from trade) 'must have been' greater than the transactions costs of concluding it. Under freedom of contract, then, trading will go on and the Pareto-improvements that trading produces will be 'locked in' until no potential gains are left that would exceed the presumable transactions costs—that is, until economic and social arrangements become 'efficient' for the time being.

What is true of contracts is, by analogy, easily but mistakenly thought to be true of conventions. Some norm would be beneficial to the group adopting it: therefore, subject only to transactions costs, it will be adopted (though it may take a generation or two before it is firmly in place). However, this is treating the group as if it were a single individual who bears the full consequences of his actions, reaping all their benefits and incurring their full cost. As long as he is aware of them and anticipates them fairly correctly, he can probably be relied upon to take the beneficial course of action. Extrapolating from the individual to the group, however, is an arbitrary step. It is a mark of functionalist social science which tacitly assumes that norms and practices are adopted *because* they have a useful function and are 'needed'.[1] The use of money facilitates exchange, it is a gain over barter, which is sometimes thought to be all we need now to understand why it arose and became a near-universal practice. (Carl Menger, who presented money as a tacit social convention, of course understood well enough that it was not obvious why any individual should agree to give up his goods in exchange for little metal tokens.) If only the usefulness of a convention sufficed for it to be adopted, some of the most difficult political problems would evaporate, and so might politics.

If there is no group mind, treating a community as if it were motivated and acted as a single individual, amounts to the 'fallacy of composition'. It is a fallacy because it ignores the crucial difference between the benefit to each member of a group

---

[1] Harold Demsetz remarks that the existence of 'the institution of private property, which attempts to exclude non-purchasers . . . is probably due in part to its great practicality in revealing the social values upon which to base solutions to scarcity problems'. (H. Demsetz, 'The Exchange and Enforcement of Property Rights', *Journal of Law and Economics*, 1964, p. 21.) The usefulness of (private) property to society is clear enough. What is sometimes problematical is to show why particular individuals choose to act in ways that will cause the conventions of property to emerge. Social utility may well leave them cold.

if most of them act in the common interest, and the benefit to a single member if *he* acts in the common interest, whatever the others do. In the latter case, too little of the marginal benefit produced by the single individual may accrue to him, most of it going to the rest of the group. He just may have sufficient incentive to act in the common interest, but this has to be found to be so, and cannot simply be assumed. Thus, knowing that it is rational for the group as a whole to act in a certain way is very far from knowing that its individual members will find it rational so to act. The potential social benefit from a convention is not a sufficient reason for its adoption and survival.

Explaining conventions is more difficult than explaining contracts. Moreover, the greater difficulty of understanding them is a hint that they *are* more difficult altogether, and, unlike contracts, do not have the apparent capacity to capture all available gains and hence to lead to Pareto-optimality. However, the move from a mere Pareto-improvement to a Pareto-optimal one—that is, from a good to the best solution—would usually require recourse to collective choice and coercion. *Whether a 'coerced optimum' is a sensible category at all* is obviously problematical (and will be touched upon in Chapter 6).

2. The Emergence of Conventions

(a) Self-enforcing Norms

The first person to cross a field under freshly fallen snow has no choice about bearing the pains of breaking a path;[1] if he must cross he cannot but trudge in virgin snow.[2] The next comer can either cross in the path broken by the first, or cross in virgin snow. Keeping to the path is almost certainly his dominant alternative. As the path gets better trodden with every successive passage, its advantage over virgin snow increases. It becomes a conspicuous norm, and a firm convention to adhere to it will be adopted by those who have to cross the field. Even after a fresh fall of snow, it is likely that the same path will be broken again.

---

[1] The example of the path in the snow is I. M. Kirzner's in his 'Knowledge Problems and Their Solutions', *Cultural Dynamics*, Vol. III., 1, 1990.

[2] He may cunningly hide behind a tree and wait till someone else comes and breaks a path, but the wait may cost him more than the effort of pioneering a way across the field.

This is so regardless of whether or not the path is an optimal one. It may have been the shortest way across for the person who first broke it, but not for later-comers who have different destinations, for whom, all in all, a different path would be shorter. Nevertheless, it will pay them to stick to the sub-optimal path, for none could benefit individually from being the first to break a better one—though if one were broken, they would all want to use it.[1]

The path-in-the-snow case is one where every individual from first to last, from pioneer to copycat, has the same individually best solution (which may not be collectively best for all that). Moreover, the more people adopt it, the stronger becomes the incentive for additional people to adopt it, too, until no random deviant is left. Whenever the same type of problem crops up, the same firm convention to deal with it is likely to emerge; the convention, moreover, will be self-enforcing, for no one could benefit from being the first to abandon it.

Conformity to the norm in these conventions dominates deviation. Language and money are major conventions of this type; fragile at first, they reinforce themselves over time. 'Exogenous' geographical and political barriers are probably necessary to stop their spread and to permit separate languages, separate monies to subsist.

Certain conventions are self-enforcing, too, *once they have emerged* and taken on a critical mass, but their emergence is more fortuitous. The seven-day week is a possible example.[2] Why is it seven days and not six or five, and why is it the same for practically everybody? Suppose countrymen need periodically to cease their labours and come to town in order to meet and trade. Each can do best if he comes on a day when the most people come. Some would prefer to come every three days, others every six, 10 and so forth. Random 'bunching' of town-going will soon show up as each person comes to town at his preferred frequency. Anyone who notices the bunching tendency, faint as it may be, might find it best to exploit it and come

---

[1] *Cf.* Kirzner, *op. cit.*, p. 42.

[2] Its solution, as well as solutions to other types of co-ordination problems, is worked out in A. Schotter, *The Economic Theory of Social Institutions*, Cambridge: CUP, 1981.

to town on the day bunching seems likely—that is, when he expects to meet and trade with the most people. The initial bunching will therefore snowball, reinforce itself and become a standard frequency, a norm. Seven days may become the standard because the first few random bunches happened to show up roughly every seven days; it may be, however, that five days or nine would have suited more people better. Once, however, a good solution emerged in the form of the seven-day week, no one can rationally do anything to bring about the even better five or nine-day week. Nor is any enforcement needed to ensure survival of the seven-day one.

In yet another type of choice-co-ordination problem, a convention would benefit all once it was established, and no one could do better by deviating from it. Yet its emergence cannot be expected from purely chance phenomena. Take the problem of rights-of-way and of the avoidance of bumping into each other. If two vehicles meet head on, and there is no traffic rule, who gives way is a matter of negotiation, possibly backed by intimidation, bargaining power. Each solution is a separately negotiated 'contract' for avoiding collision.

If there are many similar bargaining problems, there are good reasons for the parties to agree on solutions that follow precedent in a mechanistic way. Contract, in other words, tends to fade into custom. Instead of each head-on encounter being resolved on a case-by-case basis, custom (such as passing on the left, overtaking on the right, etc.) will come to be recognised. Apart from the economy of 'negotiating costs' that are won when encountering others who recognise the same custom (an economy that rises in line with the proportion of drivers adhering to it), there is a more than proportional penalty attaching to deviation once a critical mass of drivers adhere: for beyond that point, those who do follow the custom tend to assume that others do, too, and do not stop or slow down to make sure.

From then on, conforming to the same traffic rule is best for all, and it solidifies into a firm convention all by itself. It is self-enforcing within narrow limits: reasonable men will obey its main provisions most of the time, infringing them some of the time, and only unreasonable men will infringe them most of the time.

Reasoning about the causes of the emergence of a civilising

convention, such as the right-of-way, is equally applicable to the understanding of the main springs of the common law. The father of custom is contract; precedent eases negotiation and agreement, or makes it altogether unnecessary; custom economises on contracts;[1] past a critical degree of conformity, deviation involves a growing risk of collision.

Collision, the clash of incompatible choices, 'bumping' into each other's interests is the central subject of the law of torts and of property. The origin and evolution of the common law is, of course, a vast, untidy and imperfectly known story and it would be ludicrous to suggest that 'using precedent to economise on contracting' is the one rationally designed key to it that will make it suddenly as simple as an open book. At least, however, the key helps us visualise an imaginary yet logical reconstruction of how and why something like the common law would have emerged if it (or in civil law countries, offsprings of Roman law) had not come about as it in fact did.

(b) Enforcement-Dependent Conventions

For conventions to be part of the liberal framework of *voluntary* curbs on individual choice, they must be *ultimately* self-enforcing, even if they are not proximately so. When is a convention 'ultimately' self-enforcing? I propose, as a possible definition, a set of interdependent conventions where the individual actions required for enforcing one convention in the set (the main or first-order convention) result from conformity with another (the satellite or second-order convention), and the latter 'convention-to-enforce' is itself self-enforcing. (In a more complex set, the second-order or satellite convention-to-enforce may, in turn, depend on its own third-order satellite to enforce the second-order one, and so on, producing a regress. The whole would be ultimately self-enforcing if the last one in the chain was self-enforcing.) The satellite convention telling people to help

---

[1] The traffic light is surely the ultimate contract-economising device. It replaces *ad hoc* agreements at intersections with an automatic mechanism that saves time and argument. If they stop at red and go at green, drivers need neither to haggle, nor to risk collision. That most people would voluntarily obey traffic lights is likely. That enough would voluntarily contribute to the installation of traffic lights is more difficult to prove, but so is the proposition that not enough would do so.

enforce the main one, is a Pareto-improvement if it can be obtained by the agreement of some and the acquiescence of the rest. Although not all may agree to enforce it, the satellite convention will work if some critical proportion does. It suffices then that the free-riding rest do not oppose it, do not undo the efforts of the enforcers, and hence need not be overruled by the authority of collective choice.

There are two ways in which a non-self-enforcing convention may stand in need of enforcement. It may need it to survive, and it may need it to fulfil its purpose. The two needs overlap but do not coincide. A convention that unravels obviously ceases to serve any useful purpose, but the inverse need not be true, for a convention disobeyed by many may well continue to be respected for a very long time by the rest, though it has lost its utility. Queueing seems to be an example of the first, conventions against injury to life, limb and property of the second.

Queueing, as I have argued earlier (Ch. 4, 3 (5), above, p. 70), is behaviour that obeys a self-evident first principle. First come, first on the bus, at the serving counter, or wherever priorities are *not* allocated by *desert* nor by *willingness and ability to pay*, is a plausible basis for an apparently simple convention which, however, has a treacherous, perverse incentive structure. The more people conform to it, the greater the advantage anyone can reap from not conforming. Either the absolute length of the queue, or the proportion of those queueing relative to those who will mill around, may act as the trigger for quitting the queue. At the trigger level, the respect of the marginal queuer for the first-come principle is just overcome by the attractions of queue-jumping, and the more are seen to jump, the greater the urge the others will feel to jump, too, rather than be bypassed. Therefore a queue that starts to unravel tends to unravel altogether. What is true of a given queue at a given bus stop or ticket window is likely to be true, at one remove, for the whole convention of queueing. If too many queues collapse into milling around, the norm itself will unravel and the civilisation in question will, at least temporarily, lose its capacity to benefit from 'first-come-first-served'.

The 'cost' of enforcing queueing is probably modest. Often, it will suffice for one or two indignant voices in the queue to cry shame and admonish the queue-jumper, though dealing with the thick-skinned may call for more energetic dissuasion. However, while it is better and morally more satisfying for most if the queue survives, it is not obvious that any single individual standing in it will be moved to participate in enforcing its discipline, especially as there is always a chance that others will do it instead of him. His decision, then, if regarded in the narrowest utility-maximising perspective, is mainly a function of the likelihood he attaches to others assuming the task of protecting the queue. Since this proposition is symmetrical, with its inverse being no less valid, there must be some benign equilibrating tendency, by which a correctly perceived risk that the necessary discipline might *not* be enforced by others, will increase one's own willingness to expend effort to uphold it.[1] The perverse incentive held out by the convention: it pays to jump the queue *if enough others are queueing*, is thus happily countered by the constructive incentive structure of the satellite convention about enforcement: it pays to discourage the offender *if it looks that others will not do it*.

Respect for the life, limb and property of others is a norm some quite high proportion of a community's members must conform to, in order for the purpose of the convention, that is, a general sense of secure rights, to be served. The second-order convention to enforce this very important convention must itself be a robust one. Robustness is ensured if the incentive to enforce consists, not merely in saving the intended benefit of the convention—that is, having secure rights all round—but in an additional, direct and private return reserved to the enforcer.

Historically, this ingenious combination was achieved by the ancient conventional practice of buying off retaliation for torts. The lever first giving rise to this convention appears to have been the duty of the blood feud. Except for families and clans of very unequal strength, it was in the prudential interest of both the

---

[1] Enforcement is a public good that benefits all if some will contribute to its cost. The risk of losing the benefit altogether if too few happen to contribute, serves as an incentive to contribute; for the reward of doing so is the benefit divided by the risk the contribution insures against. The subjective evaluation of the benefit and of the risk by each divides the population in two camps, contributors and free-riders, and is at the heart of the possibility of providing public goods voluntarily.

offending and the offended side to limit its perilous escalation by 'capping' the duty by a tariff: a tooth for a tooth but not two teeth—and it is easy to imagine how such a tariff would, by the force of precedent, become a customary standard. The tort from then on did not have to be *revenged*. It could be *compensated*, according to customary scales, by so many cattle, so many days of labour and, as the use of money spread more widely, by pecuniary fines.

The interest of the plaintiff in actually getting the compensation served to enhance the incentive to make the effort of enforcement, or have allies make it. For the return on this effort was not only, as is generally the case in conventions, the public good of a beneficial norm upheld, but also the private good of cattle, labour or money. These private goods beckoning at the end of an enforcing action were, one way or another, persuasive arguments in favour of mutual aid by fellow villagers, guild members or other peers of the plaintiff.

(c) Legitimate Coercion

Individual interest, then, seems capable in a large enough variety of problem situations to generate the individual actions that will cause the conventions of a civilised social framework to emerge and solidify. The underlying choices are wholly voluntary, steered by no central will at co-ordination. Some of the conventions need satellite conventions for their enforcement. These satellites, some of which may work more reliably than others, can also be shown to be the unco-ordinated, spontaneous products of individually rational choices. If this is the case, the coercion they exert to protect a convention is, within strictly liberal doctrine, a legitimate one.

This follows from the 'ultimately self-enforcing' nature of the complex conventions whose satellite, enforcing convention is itself self-enforcing. If the latter were in its turn *also* dependent on enforcement, it could never be shown that the coercion it took to enforce it could have been agreed by some of those concerned without being opposed by any of the rest. In other words, it might very well not be a Pareto-improvement. On the other hand, the main convention would collapse, hence cease to benefit both conformers and would-be deviant free-riders, if the satellite convention did not back it up.[1] No principle of the liberal order is violated by the coercion exerted by such a satellite convention, and it can be taken as legitimate. The presumption is that its introduction would be rationally unopposed even by those who, at one time or another, might expect to be subjected to it; for the latter can only derive abusive free-rider benefit from the main convention if it is there to be abused, and does not collapse for lack of enforcement.

3. The Source of Rights

Next to conventions, choice must be circumscribed by rights. Contract is their obvious, self-evident source, because only contracts provide proof that the correlative obligation has been *agreed to* by the obligor, hence its existence does not depend on controversial claims.

Conventions emerge without being willed. They are Pareto-improvements without necessarily being optimal. Contracts are negotiated and concluded deliberately, and they are Pareto-optimal. Being voluntary, willed and non-imposed, and improving the lot of the parties, contracts are a quintessentially liberal institution, and deserve particular consideration.

It is easy to concede that contracts are an uncontestable source of rights. Are they, however, their only source? Are there any non-contractual rights?

Enough has been said above (Chapter 3) about the distinction

---

[1] In game-theoretical language, if the main convention in question has the pay-off structure of a 'prisoners' dilemma', taken in isolation it would have a Pareto-inferior solution (the convention would fail to yield benefits). Combined with its enforcing satellite, it would enable the players to move to a Pareto-superior solution by virtue of the threat to the would-be deviant that would induce him not to deviate.

Producing the threat is, in turn, Pareto-superior for some of the players in the satellite 'game', whose two central pay-offs consist of the risk-adjusted values of preserving the main convention and its benefits at some cost, *or* losing them if it collapses but incurring no costs in its enforcement. The central pay-offs are straddled by two more extreme pay-offs, costly failure and blissful free ride.

This is a game of 'hawk and dove' where some will normally find it rational to play hawk, others dove. The doves will do their civic duty of enforcing the convention; the hawks will parasitically benefit. Given their expectations about each other's actions, neither hawks nor doves can profitably change the rôle they have adopted.

between is- and ought-rights, and about the logical equivalence between a right and the obligation that permits it to be exercised, to show why it is more pertinent to rephrase the question, and ask: Are there any non-contractual obligations?[1]

Any quick answer would prove, on close examination, to be rash. Nevertheless, if there is an answer, it would presumably proceed along predictable lines. Somebody's non-contractual right is one involving somebody else's obligation to which the obligor has not agreed and would prefer not to owe. Such obligations are unrequited or, at all events, insufficiently compensated for (for otherwise they would have been voluntarily entered into).

There is one clear case where the obligor can be placed under an unrequited obligation without unjustly harming his interests: when the obligation in question does not deprive him of any liberty, nor of any right, that *he would otherwise have had*. The obligation to respect the property of another acquired by 'finders' keepers' would be of this kind; the wider obligation to respect the *status quo* can be derived along the same lines (though there are alternative ways of deriving it, too).

In any other case, imposing an obligation on someone without his agreement, and in the really important cases in spite of his explicit dissent, is a *prima facie* injustice. If it has a moral excuse, it must be sought in the greater merit of the correlative right that its imposition permits to be exercised. In a less rigorous and more diffuse way, however, one may seek to justify the obligation by appeals to overall utility, the public interest, the general will; such appeals are more difficult to challenge because of their very vagueness.

In any event, however, justifying a non-contractual obligation (going beyond the kind that has no opportunity cost) is finally reducible to a weighing of the good of one category or class of persons—the proposed new right-holders—against that of another—the newly designated obligors. The weights to be set against one another are not ascertainable facts ('data'). Nor are they the logical consequences of agreed truths. Instead, they are moral judgements which can always be opposed by other moral judgements. The judgement between opposing judgements may,

---

[1] As the reader may recall, I distinguish 'obligation' from 'duty'.

with luck and perseverance, be obtained by persuasion. Failing that, it must be produced by the use of authority backed, if need be, by preponderant power.

Obligations imposed on unwilling obligors, therefore, have a status that is, to put it as soberly as one can, not comparable to the status of contractual obligations. The corresponding rights are likewise incomparable. Contractual rights are sure to exist if, and because, even those *unfavourably affected* by them, namely the other parties to partly executed contracts, must acknowledge that they do in the face of evidence that a contract exists. Perhaps non-contractual rights exist, too, but the claim that they do tends to be made by those who would benefit from them, and their epistemological as well as their ethical standing is very different. It is a source of confusion that they go under the same name.

4. The Freedom of Contract

The particular respect which, for these reasons, contracts deserve in the eyes of strict liberals, strikes loose liberals as little better than metaphysical obscurantism or plain superstition. Like property, loose liberalism regards contract, too, as a social *privilege*, in the gift of the state because, again like property, it is enforced by 'society' and would crumble without the state's sustaining will.

If the appeal to a discretionary favour done by the state (or 'society') to would-be contracting parties is disallowed as bordering on the preposterous, there are a number of other standard arguments to the effect that contracts cannot, or must not, or need not, be allowed to create rights and obligations at the sole will of the parties. What these arguments really assert is that the freedom of contract is not a 'liberty'—that is, a faculty that we suppose to exist until proof is brought to the contrary.[1]

---

[1] To quote Dworkin again: 'What can be said, for instance, in favor of the *right to liberty* of contract sustained by the Supreme Court in the famous *Lochner* case, and later regretted, not only by the court, but by liberals generally? I cannot think of any argument that a political decision to limit such a right . . . is antecedently likely to give effect to external preferences . . . If, as I think, no such argument can be made out, then the alleged *right* does not exist; in any case there can be no inconsistency in denying that it exists while warmly defending the *right to other liberties*.' (R. Dworkin, *op. cit.*, p. 278 (my italics).)

[*Contd. on p. 94*]

Failing some such general claim, particular grounds are found for taking the institution of contract down a peg or two.

(a) Efficiency

Strict liberal doctrine cannot but hold that contracting is free because no right to the contrary can be (or at least none has been) proved, and that contracts must be honoured because promises must be kept. As a second string to its contractual bow, the doctrine holds that contracts must be free and honoured because they are Pareto-optimal and we value the economic efficiency implied in that condition. To cut this second string (the target of those who do not think much of the force of the first anyway), attempts can be made to show that in certain circumstances freely negotiated contracts have inefficient effects and it would be better if they were not enforced.

In one such attempt, Patrick Atiyah[1] seeks to justify the view (of which he is a prominent defender[2]) that freedom of contract is a much overrated value. Its inefficiency comes to the surface

---

There is neither room nor need now to go into the peculiar argument that political decisions to curtail liberties (or rights?) are *prima facie* justified unless they pander to 'external preferences', nor into whether 'external preferences' really mean what Dworkin wishes them to mean. It suffices for the present to note that preferences to curtail the freedom of contract, such as concern for the poor, envy of the rich, regulatory meddlesomeness, are to have free rein, while preferences to curtail other liberties, such as racial prejudice, sexual bigotry, or artistic philistinism, are to be disallowed. Clearly, if racial prejudice is 'external', so is envy or concern for the poor: if one is disallowed, so should the others be.

It turns out, on inspection, that what matters for this argument is not whether preferences to curtail liberties are 'external' or 'internal', but whether we wish to defend what they would curtail. We rule them out if they would curtail freedom of expression, *avant-garde* art or unorthodox sexual tastes, and we rule them in if they would curtail freedom of contract.

A more above-board and less tortuous short cut would be simply to state that we do not believe that there is a universal argument (such as the burden-of-proof distinction between liberty and right set out in Chapter 3) in favour of liberties in general. We can then pick and choose among them on *ad hoc* grounds. The laboured and unsustainable criterion of 'external' preferences becomes mercifully redundant, and can be safely forgotten.

[1] P. Atiyah, 'The Theoretical Basis of Contract Law—An English Perspective', *International Review of Law and Economics*, Vol. 1, 1981.

[2] P. Atiyah, *The Rise and Fall of Freedom of Contract*, Oxford: OUP, 1979.

in certain contracts which would force the parties to carry out bargains on terms agreed in the past; it is quite possible that a bargain was an efficient, value-maximising allocation of the resources involved at the time, but by the time the contract is to be executed, it is not one any more. This case is effectively demolished by Franco Romani who proves[1] that *if* invalidating a contract permitted to avoid an inefficient outcome, it would be avoided anyway, even if the contract were enforceable, since it would by definition pay both parties to rectify the inefficiency by re-contracting and ending up with a new bargain that was Pareto-optimal at the time it was executed.

On the other hand, as Romani puts it, if what the critics of contract really want to say is that 'any exchange is inefficient insofar as a party may subsequently change his mind',[2] their charge neither has nor requires an answer.

(b) Externality

In considering how the harm principle can be stretched until its freedom-constraining effects extend over harms that violate no right nor convention, but are simply negative externalities not compensable in common law (Ch.2, 4(d)), reference was made to 'market failure' in the form of purported differences between private and social cost, or benefit. Freedom of contract allows the parties to reach a mutually beneficial agreement whose side-effect imposes costs on others without the latter's agreement. If this is the case, contractual freedom may be neither efficient nor just. The two charges need separate answers.

If a contract between two parties damages a third, a test of whether the total effect is efficient is offered by the freedom of contract. Suppose that A and B conclude a bargain that confers on them benefits jointly worth £100, and imposes some cost on C. If avoiding the cost is worth more than £100 to him, and no mutually profitable contracts are hindered by the legal system, C can contract with A and B, paying them £101 if they desist from their bargain. The new bargain is efficient. If avoiding the cost is

---

[1] F. Romani, 'Some Notes on the Economic Analysis of Contract Law', in T. Daintith and G. Teubner (eds.), *Contract and Organisation*, Berlin and New York: Walter de Gruyter, 1986.

[2] *Ibid.*, p. 128.

worth less than £100 to *C*, the old bargain stands and was efficient. (The argument rests on the same theorem as Romani's in (a) above.) In either case, efficiency is tough luck on *C*; however, the last word on his luck has not yet been said.

The original contract allowed to stand between *A* and *B*, it may be argued, may nevertheless have been inefficient if transactions costs prevented *C* from re-contracting with *A* and *B*. However, if transactions costs are too high to allow *C* profitably to bribe *A* and *B* to desist from their bargain, then making them desist would not be efficient because it would cost too much. This is a truism that follows from the definition of contracts and their transactions costs, but it will have to do until it can be shown that non-contractual ways (for example, government regulation) of replacing an old bargain benefiting *A* and *B*, by an amended one taking account of *C*'s interest, is somehow cheaper. Until and unless this is shown, transactions costs must be regarded as no less genuine 'bads' than the externality we could avoid or compensate if transactions costs allowed it to be done efficiently.[1] One may speculate, albeit without any great confidence, that if legal impediments and uncertainties were removed, and the costly state monopoly of contract enforcement were replaced by competing arrangements, transactions costs might be reduced and present less of an obstacle to the contractual buying-out of externalities or to their compensation.

It may be efficient, but is it just to allow *A* and *B* to act in a way that imposes a cost on innocent *C*, that he can only avoid by fully or more than fully compensating *A* and *B* for not doing what is profitable for them but costly to him? Can it possibly be just, for instance, that the burden of keeping the air breathable should fall, not on the fume-spewing factory, but on those downwind from it who want to breathe?

Such answer as strict liberalism can offer is in several parts. Truly offensive externalities may come to be regarded as torts, entailing liability to compensate the victim, and strict liberalism has no quarrel with conventions against torts that spontaneously emerge, nor with their evolution, reflected in the common law,

---

[1] *Cf.* the incisive essay by C. J. Dahlman, 'The Problems of Externality', in T. Cowen (ed.), *The Theory of Market Failure*, Fairfax, Va.: George Mason University Press, 1988, which takes the matter very much further than I can do here.

by which liability for externalities is assigned to one party (e.g. the polluter) rather than another (the victim).

If, however, such is not the case, and the downwind residents can show no right to clean air, the situation is 'morally arbitrary'. The manufacturer's interest in the most economical process that, however, emits noxious fumes is opposed to the residents' interest in clean air and it is not immediately obvious why one should give way to the other.[1]

As in some other morally arbitrary situations, 'first-come-first-served' suggests the beginnings of an answer. Whoever is in possession, and content with the *status quo*, should not be liable for the cost of changing it. Residents enjoying clean air should not be liable to suffer the inconvenience of foul air produced by a new chemical plant nor have to bribe the manufacturer to go away and put the plant elsewhere. On the other hand, if it is they who want to change the *status quo* and get rid of the air-fouling plant which has been there for some time, the latter should presumably count as the first-comer and it is for the residents to bribe it to go away or change its technology if the value they put on cleaner air makes it worth their while to do so.

(c) The Cheshire Cat

Freedom of contract, no less than the freedom of all other choices, is limited by both the availability and the admissibility of options. Most appeals to curtail it are made on grounds of admissibility; because certain classes of contracts may have inefficient or unjust results, it is proposed to rule them out or

---

[1] The solution is not obvious for more than one reason. The choice is not between putting the burden on the manufacturer or on the householders. It is between putting it on the householders on the one hand, and on the manufacturer, his employees, suppliers, and the consumers of his product on the other hand. If the latter, it is impossible to tell who ends up paying what. Compensation payable by the polluting manufacturer to the victims (or the cost of changing over to a non-polluting process), has its proximate incidence on the manufacturer's profit, on the prices he charges, and on the incomes he pays to his employees and suppliers, depending on all the relevant elasticities of supply and demand. However, the ultimate incidence in a new, post-compensation general equilibrium is unpredictable in practice though it is 'knowable', in a purely formal and operationally irrelevant way, in theory. At all events, it is impossible to tell whether it is the 'rich' or the 'poor' who end up paying for cleaner air.

control their terms. A more radical attack on freedom of contract, however, takes the very availability of contract options as its target. If certain options are put out of reach, they cannot be contracted for: nobody can sell what is not his to sell.

The simplest kind of anti-contract proposition is one we had occasion to note in earlier contexts. It is that people do not *own* the assets under their control, not even such personal endowments as their intelligence, talent and capacity for effort. The distribution of personal endowments is 'morally arbitrary' because no one has merited his parents; that of transferable assets is a matter of the institutional environment which is society's handiwork and is up to society to leave in place or to change.

Somewhat more moderate in appearance, but equivalent in its effect, is the proposition that people do own their assets (including their inseparable personal endowments) but are not entitled to freedom of contract over them as a consequence.

This view gets no doubt quite unintended support from the modern functionalist analysis of property rights—an analysis that it is singularly easy to misunderstand in good faith and abuse in bad. Unobjectionably, this branch of economics 'partitions' ownership into functionally distinct property rights. A 'bundle' of such rights attaches to an asset. A piece of land, as Armen Alchian puts it, is subject to a variety of rights which can belong to separate persons:

> '*A* may possess the right to grow wheat on it, *B* may possess the right to walk across it, *C* may possess the right to dump ashes and smoke on it, *D* may possess the right to fly an airplane over it . . . The rights can be partitioned, divided and reallocated on a temporary—or even on a permanent—basis.'[1]

There are 'bailments, easements, leases, franchises, inheritances, etc.'.[2] Like sticks bound together in a bundle, each right can be unbundled—separated from the others without ceasing to be a stick.

When, however, does the bundle of sticks cease to be a

---

[1] A. Alchian, 'Some Economics of Property Rights', *Economic Forces At Work*, Indianapolis: Liberty Press, 1977, pp. 132-33.

[2] *Ibid.*, p. 135.

bundle? As the various property rights making it up are one by one detached in voluntary transactions or curtailed or redistributed by political choices, the bundle gets thinner. But is there a decisive, core 'stick' whose removal would lead us to say that now there is no bundle any more, just a stray stick or two? If no stick is special and decisive—that is, if no right is essential to ownership—the process of detaching its component rights can go on, in no particular order, until ownership fades away like the Cheshire Cat.

Viewing *all* rights attaching to an asset as equally detachable, with none being ultimately inseparable from ownership of the asset, allows the freedom of contract to be denied while professing respect for title to ownership.

At some point in the process of dissecting ownership, the right to transfer its component rights may itself be removed like any of the others. If it is true that this right is no different in kind from ownership's other prerogatives, one can take freedom of contract away and still have ownership: at least the grin of the Cheshire Cat would linger on after its body has faded away.

From this view of ownership, it is a natural step to affirm that while owners may be allowed, as a matter of social expediency, to sell their goods and services, their assets and the products they yield, the *terms* on which they may do it are for 'society' to fix. The upshot of this line of reasoning is worth close inspection:

'... *owning* a talent is one thing, and *benefiting* from it in a scheme of social co-operation is quite another. What, then, does a person own when he owns a talent? ... I guess what he owns is a capacity that he can, as it were, "plug in" or relate to any of an array of possible social structures to produce various levels of benefit, for himself and others'.[1]

Whoever penetrates this verbiage about 'relating to possible structures', can only mutter 'so there!'. Whoever foolishly believed that owning entailed benefiting, and that the levels of benefit to self and others were matters of the reciprocal valuation of what we offered to each other in mutually agreed exchanges, must now see that this is not how ownership works at all. It works by 'relating to a structure in an array'.

---

[1] J. Waldron, *The Right to Private Property*, Oxford: OUP, 1988, pp. 405-6 (my italics).

The discoverer of these novel relations goes on to explain that ownership and benefiting from ownership need not be related *at all*. In an environmentalist society that prohibited mining, a gifted prospector would own his talent but could not make a living out of it. This, of course, is a truism that follows directly from mining being ruled out. The problem of benefiting from knowledge about mining is assumed away by supposing a society where the knowledge has been made useless to others. What, however, is the position of the prospector and the mine-owner when everybody else in a society is 'allowed by society' to use locally mined minerals?

We are asked to believe that 'self-ownership confers *no right* whatsoever to exercise one's talents *for one's own benefit*'[1] since the possibility of benefiting, as the example of prohibited mining shows, is entirely contingent on having the kind of social framework that condones it.

Such reasoning is specious. Alternative social frameworks, one ruling out mining, the other murder, the third something else, are not a matter of pure contingency; nor is the prohibition of using a product or service a matter of chance. If, as Waldron goes on to suggest, there are independent moral reasons for having a certain sort of society, one that places *fewer* prohibitions on reciprocally agreeable exchanges of goods or services its members wish to obtain, is surely less a result of historical contingencies, and likely to have stronger moral principles on its side, than one putting *more* prohibitions in their way.

But there is a more decisive reason for rejecting the thesis that it is up to society to allow, disallow or fix the level of the benefit derived from ownership. Even if no moral or efficiency reasons militated one way or the other for kinds of society, and the prospector's nose, the mine, or any other asset and talent could indeed be made valueless by historically contingent prohibitions, it would still not be the case that the terms of the remaining contracts, too, were for society to fix. One could concede that they were without further ado if, but only if, nothing *else* fixed them, or if whatever else fixed them had to be rejected as illegitimate or inefficient, so that social discretion could take its place by default. Since, however, the terms of exchanges are

---

[1] Waldron, *op. cit.*, p. 408 (my italics).

determined by the best interest and judgement of those wishing to make them, and nothing permits us to condemn the relevant interests as illegitimate nor to conclude that the exchange process is inefficient, it is hard to see why it should be taken for granted that 'society' can, without raising grave questions of legitimacy, override what its members jointly and severally choose to arrange among themselves.

In the last resort, it is of course always possible to claim some kind of overriding legitimacy for society by simply postulating that its interests, judgements and decisions take precedence over those of its individual members: such a postulate would be a take-it-or-leave-it axiom, not to be argued for. It would, however, have a logical content incompatible with private property. I shall revert to this point presently.

For the believer in social discretion,

'individual income and wealth is a product of social conditions rather than the fruit of individual effort, in the first place.'[1]

Admittedly, a good or a service is what it is thanks to the anonymous and untraceable contributions of countless contemporaries and their ancestors (going back to Noah) to our civilisation, to the stock of capital, knowledge and the orderly working of institutions. It would be foolish to contest the truth of this platitude. One cannot deduce from it, however, that when a good is exchanged, only some part of its exchange value should be conceded to its owner, some other and presumably far greater part being handed over to 'society' whose 'product' it chiefly is. Still less does it mean that the parts due to particular members of society are indeterminate, and are to be determined by social discretion. Economics, and at a more general and abstract level the theory of rational decisions, has long ago shown that there is no indeterminacy, and no perplexity about what is due to whom. If we all seek to choose rationally and leave sub-optimal options in favour of better ones, any person's income, the value of his efforts and of his assets are all determined by their *marginal* contribution to the interests, preferences and concerns of all others, and *vice versa*. There is nothing wrong with imputing some part, however large, of *total* reciprocal contributions to past

---

[1] Feinberg, *op. cit.*, p. 16.

generations since Noah, history or society, as long as it is not proposed, as a purported logical consequence, to pay a corresponding part of the income flows we generate, likewise to past generations since Noah, history or society. Noah and his descendants have been rewarded for their contributions once before—when they made them. Total contribution (if the notion really means anything) is not to be confused with marginal value-product, and need not be rewarded twice over.

Jeremy Waldron, to whom we owe the luminous explication of (self)-ownership being the capacity 'to relate to any of an array of possible social structures to produce various levels of benefit', seems persuaded that curtailment of the freedom of contract does not undermine the intrinsic purpose, the 'point' of the institution of contracting. Its point is preserved, for the parties adjust their expectations to, for example, a given fiscal régime or to any other requirements that may be set by a society 'committed to the ideals of rights, liberty and justice'. Society sets these fiscal and other limits, and people 'seem able to carry on transferring goods *freely within the constraints* it imposes'.[1] But the italicised words merely iterate a tautology. Of course they do transfer 'freely within the constraints', just as the caged beast moves freely within its cage (especially if it has 'adjusted its expectations to it'). Constraints *mean* that you move 'freely' *within* but only within them, and it is nothing short of fatuous to find that people seem indeed able to do so. Evidently they do, but does their ability to transfer property 'within constraints' excuse the given constraints?—or does it rather suggest some others?—and does it prove anything about particular constraints being legitimate, efficient, and consistent with the preservation of the whole 'point' of property?

Here I can finally revert to the 'bundle of sticks' conception of ownership as a collection of independently detachable property rights. Take once again the piece of unencumbered land owned by a person in freehold. Under freedom of contract, he can transfer the right to farm the land to *A* while reserving a right of way across it to *B*, borrow money against a mortgage granted to *C*, sell to *D* the right to the rents payable by *A*, and so on. As long as there are rights left that he has not transferred, or as long as he

---

[1] Waldron, *op. cit.*, p. 436 (my italics).

transferred all but only temporarily, with some or all reverting to him in due course, he effectively retains the residual equity and *the right to transfer rights*. Despite appearances, the grin of the Cheshire Cat is still there.

If, however, he has sold a perpetual and transferable tenancy to *A* and a perpetual right to the rental to *D*, he has *used up* his right to transfer rights, and has ceased to be the owner. Two new assets will have been created, the perpetual tenancy subject to a rent, and the stream of rentals, and two owners *A* and *D*.

The right to transfer rights, then, is the only one within the bundle of detachable rights that is an essential, non-separable constituent of ownership. It is plainly a necessary condition for the strict-liberal Exclusion principle to fulfil its purpose in ensuring efficient resource allocation, and this is one source of its legitimacy. The right in question, however, is not a *right* in the rigorous, Hohfeldian sense (see Box, above, pp. 48-49, and note, above, pp. 93-94) but a *liberty*. The owner *has* freedom of contract subject to proof of rights to the contrary. Like every other liberty, it is subject to the conflicting rights of others; no one can dispose of a right owned by another.

Freedom of contract and ownership are mutually entailed and *neither has intelligible meaning without the other*; attempts to separate them end in intellectual confusion in theory, and grief in legal and economic affairs. Subordinating ownership as such to 'society's will'—to collective choice—is one thing, confining social discretion to controlling the terms of contracts while still recognising the right to private property, is another. The former is ultimately anchored to the socialist principle that individuals do not rightfully own either themselves or productive assets, only 'society' does. Such a position is quite possible; though there are what I would consider decisive arguments against it, it can be taken seriously. It rejects contractual freedom because it has already rejected personal ownership. No similar credit for consistency is due to the alternative, having-it-both-ways position that wishes to say *both* that persons are entitled to own whatever they have legally acquired, *and* that their freedom to make contracts over what they own is contingent on the 'social framework', whatever the contingence is intended to mean. This stand is self-contradictory, and clarity about these matters demands that it should be exposed as such.

6

CONSENTING
TO POLITICS

1. The Power of Collective Choice

POLITICS AT ITS MOST BASIC is the generation and execution of collective choices. As such it is an instrument of extraordinary power. It has evident potential both for great good and unpardonable bad, with a broad array of the middling-good and middling-bad in between. Depending on outlook, worldly wisdom and the lessons administered by history, some expect it to produce more good outcomes than bad; for others, this is being far too guileless. Moreover, the same outcome produced by politics may strike some as good, others as bad. Often this is the reason why the former seek to impose it on the latter. These are the two root causes of the contentiousness of politics.

Since Plato, political theory has on the whole tended to see politics as an object of hope rather than of fear. The very nature of most political doctrines is teleological, and maximising: it expects the power of collective choice to be used in the realisation of a goal, or a hierarchy of goals, and (when more of one thing means less of another) in the judicious setting of rates of trade-off between them. Facetiously, one could say that any such ambition reflects a triumph of wishful thinking over experience; yet it goes against the grain of political theory to be 'against politics'.

Strict liberalism stands apart in this respect, alone in implicitly holding that though politics need not and presumably cannot be totally negated, it should not be embraced either. It must be consented to, but only on conditions, warily and grudgingly. Moreover, consent must not be construed as irrevocable, given once and for all as in standard social contract theories. It has to be earned again and again as the case for specific kinds of collective choices is subjected to constant critical scrutiny.

This is obviously not how politics works: it is not tame by nature, it has its own built-in dynamics, and may very well not meekly content itself with limited powers and rôles, conceded only till revoked. Under strict liberalism, however, this is how politics ought to work, and the key function of a liberal order is to generate dispositions for it to work in this way.

(a) The Parameters of Collective Choice

Individual choice is unanimous in that the chooser agrees with himself. It is the limiting case of unanimity. Conversely, unanimity could be seen as generalised individual choice, with many choosers all making identical choices for themselves. Where some choose the same option and others abstain, we are of course still in the realm of unanimity. The Pareto-superiority definitionally implied in individual choice still prevails (subject to any adverse externality affecting those who have not been consulted), and continues to prevail right up to the border where unanimity stops and collective choice begins.

Collective choice is the realm where options are chosen for a group over the opposition of some part of the group. Their opposition signifies, and for lack of other independent evidence is taken to be equivalent to, the option being Pareto-inferior and dominated by at least one other option for the dissenters. While many kinds of groups are capable of making collective choices, the most interesting one is the full-fledged political society. Unlike lesser groups, the choices made for it are made with sovereign authority, and cannot be appealed against to any higher power.[1]

---

[1] The sovereign authority may, for particular classes of decisions, delegate (not 'share') its sovereignty to some other body. Sovereignty 'delegated irrevocably' is in fact renounced, for that is what is *meant* by irrevocability. When the question of revocability is left unclear, grief is liable to ensue, as the individual states of the USA had occasion to learn, at one stage at the cost of a cruel civil war. At the time of writing, utter lack of clarity in the matter of revocability is in store for the states of the Soviet Union. The member-states of the European Community are at an early stage of transfers of sovereignty to the centre; time will tell whether such transfers will prove revocable or not.

Pushing logic at the expense of information content, one might choose to say that *all* choices are unanimous, i.e. individual; for what we call collective choice can always be broken down into a unanimous choice (by those who agree) and an adverse externality (suffered by those who do not).

But this sort of generalisation, though elegant enough, hides much that is worth revealing. For what makes collective choice distinctive is that the rationale of choosing a particular option springs from the fact that it is being chosen *both* for those who wish it to be chosen *and* for others; the very *reason why* the former want it is that it *will also be imposed on the latter.* Otherwise, there would be no point in choosing it collectively. It could be left to the individual decisions of those who wanted it, without making it binding on all in a group. In this, it differs in kind from (instead of being a special case of) individual choice. Barring altruism and envy,[1] the rationale of the latter springs from the preferences of the chooser to the exclusion of any externalities his choice imposes on others; he does not choose an option *because* it affects others. The very meaning of externalities is that they do *not* enter into the motivation of whoever causes them.

Collective choice is characterised by two parameters. One describes who is entitled to choose, who is the 'decisive subset' (or 'winning coalition') in the set the choice is made for. The other defines what options may (or may not) be chosen collectively. It is the border between the private and the public domain.

The king by himself, or 'in parliament', may decide for a whole country; or other *designated* individuals, princes of the church, army commanders or the heads of the grandest houses may do so unanimously, in consensus assisted by authority, or by voting where the weight of each vote depends on the power, wisdom or rank of him who casts it. Alternatively, the decisive subset may be made up of *anonymous* individuals who vote, the

---

[1] The altruist and the spiteful rank their options by taking account of the beneficial or adverse consequences that taking the option would have on others. This means that for the chooser, there is no externality: it is 'internalised'. The option is chosen in part *because* its effect on others is also an effect on oneself. In this, the choice of the altruist and the spiteful resembles collective choice, and could be generalised with the latter.

weight of each vote being independent of the identity of the voter. (A particular case of anonymity is one-man-one-vote: not only does each vote weigh the same, but each anonymous voter has the same number of votes, that is, one). An anonymous subset becomes decisive by virtue of its *numbers*, and not by virtue of the rank, merit, authority or wealth of the persons composing it. The smaller (relative to the whole set or to the number who vote) is the number in the subset entitled to be decisive, the easier it is to make collective choices. However, to prevent contradictory choices—one subset opting for raising the income tax, the other simultaneously for lowering it—the decisive subset must be no smaller than half the set and a tie-breaker.

When the subset entitled to be decisive is thus allowed to reach its minimum, collective choice is potentially at its most agile. It is sometimes also said to be at its most democratic, in that in this situation the minority capable of blocking the majority wish is at its maximum—nothing less than half the votes can do it. A larger decisive set—a qualified or super-majority requirement and, more ambiguously, multicameralism—makes collective choice more sluggish, since smaller blocking minorities can protect the *status quo* from any collective attempt at changing it.

Given its agility or sluggishness as determined by the requirements for decisiveness, collective choice is evidently the more potent the wider the domain of alternatives over which it may range. The domain is marked out by borders around or across three categories:

(i) some options are essentially private and are, as a matter of plain humanity, reserved for individual choice even in resolutely collectivist political régimes;

(ii) others may be left to individual choices subject, however, to collective choice choosing to override them at its discretion;

(iii) the last category is intrinsically collective. These options cannot be chosen individually, since one of their essential properties is that they would *not* be chosen by some part of the set (the 'losing coalition'). Their value for the decisive subset (the 'winning coalition') consists precisely in their becoming binding on everybody, including the 'losing coalition'.

Although for a radically democratic doctrine no option, no aspect of the *status quo* must be immune to the collective will (since the latter is a force for its own good), category (i) is hardly ever invaded in civilised régimes. Category (ii) is obviously disputed territory. As a mundane example, consider people's manifold options for spending their own money. Collective choice overrides, or rather pre-empts, some of their choices by taxing them. In principle (though of course not in practice), it can return to each the tax he paid in the form of publicly provided goods and services, so that when taxes and benefits are perfectly calibrated, no redistribution takes place. The effect is that part of their money will be spent for them but not by them, not as each chooses for himself, but as some choose for all. How large a part falls to collective choice is, remarkably enough, determined by collective choice itself.

This involves a quite singular, 'self-referring' authority to fix its own limits, which not only makes collective choice resistant to curbs, but also renders it complex, difficult to grasp; hence the simplistic and often wishful view of limited government and democratic control that pervades much political discourse, liberal and otherwise.

Category (iii), if it is anywhere (for some may dispute that it really exists), is indisputably in the collective domain since this is how it is defined. All options that may meet the definition fall into one of two types: they are either redistributive measures, where losses must be imposed on some people so that others may gain (these resemble 'zero-sum' conflicts though their actual sum need not be zero, and may not even be measurable), or they are measures of enforcement to overcome perverse incentives that would otherwise defeat mutually beneficial co-operation (these are 'positive-sum' arrangements, where the distribution of the sum gained need not involve a loss for anyone). It is the latter type that is mostly invoked in justifications of the state and of legitimate coercion.

(b) Domination
Recall the liberal axiom that the point of choice is to take the option that is not dominated by another. It is from this axiom

that the primacy of individual choice is directly derived; for only when he always chooses for himself has a person the certitude of never having to end up (through no fault of his own in lack of attention, laziness or weakness of will) with a worse option than the best available. Collective choice, by definition opposed by at least one of those on whose behalf it is made, is a *prima facie* violation of this condition. If politics is nevertheless a legitimate liberal institution, this violation must be justifiable in some cases. Under what circumstances, on what grounds can domination be justified?

One strand of thought invokes the 'positive-sum' nature of enforced co-operation; we shall return to it. All others have a common denominator: that collective choice offers better options for certain individuals, albeit at the cost of imposing worse ones on others (or barring their best ones), and the cost can be justified by the benefit. This is said to be the case:

o either because the collectively created better option is much better and the worse one only a little worse;

o or because the wellbeing of the person who is favoured (not to say 'made better off', for we are not sure that the favour has really made him better off, though it was meant to do so) is more important than that of the person who is disadvantaged, due to who they are, what they deserve, and in what particular way collective choice acts upon their situation;

o or, finally, because regardless of who was favoured over whom by how much and in what way, the change in the *status quo* was a good change and that is all that needs to be said (*fiat iustitia, pereat mundus*).

In these alternative grounds, it is not hard to detect family resemblances to utilitarianism, socialism, and often also a strong strand of aesthetically or religiously oriented thought. That such thought is metaphysical does not make it invalid or disreputable. It does, however, make it heavily 'value-dependent'. The comparisons it purports to make between persons, ways of changing their situation, and between states of affairs in general, are not quantitative assessments of greater and smaller, imprecise guesswork but ultimately still subject to the discipline of some kind of proof. They are qualitative judgements relying on the weights, values the judge himself imputes to the several elements of what are being compared.

'Comparison' is used here in two radically alien senses. In the sense of the quantitative *estimate*, the whole gamut of inter-personal comparisons of *deserts*, *utilities* or *satisfactions*, as well as comparisons of the *moral* or *aesthetic merits* of alternative states of affairs, would be stark nonsense. In the very different sense of *value-judgements*, or statements of goals and the ranks we give them, they make perfect sense and stand on their own merits.

What are these merits? Plainly, if collective choice is to be justified by the value or value-hierarchy it is harnessed to promote, a meta-judgement is needed to select and rank the values to be promoted. The meta-judgement, in turn, would depend on a meta-meta-judgement to help select it, and so forth. In any event, the determinant element will be a judgement, whether down at the cutting edge of collective choice itself or way up, at the remote doctrinal end of a regress of judgements about judgements; and the practical effect will be to allocate '*to each, the same common values*', however precious they are to some and irrelevant, irksome or positively hateful to others.

The practical effect of non-domination, on the other hand, is 'value-neutrality'. Though in a certain sense, through their formative effect upon preferences and interests, each individual choice is (or at least could be) inspired by value-judgements, they are the value-judgements of the choosers, and need not be adopted by others in order for the choice to be effective. The net result is '*to each, his own values*'. Non-domination, in other words, is tantamount to the non-imposition of any common values, common goals, common *maximands*. Hence it is incompatible with a political system whose purpose is the promotion of stipulated values and the pursuit of specific goals. It is incompatible even with the pursuit of freedom itself.

This paradox is not a genuine one. Its resolution lies in the recognition that freedom is not a goal that can be pursued by the instrument of collective choices. If anything, freedom is the absence of such pursuit.

(c) Agnosticism

Critics of value-neutrality, excusably enough, accuse it of indifference to values, since it would effectively leave values to look after themselves. However it may be dressed up, the alternative is worse than indifferent, for it would use the political authority to force some people to yield the right of way to the values or goals of others, without there being any clear indication that the former have consented to coercion on *this* ground. In the polar case, it is to enslave them in the service of a cause, however ennobling, as the totalitarian state would do, or to save their own souls with fire and iron in the manner of the militant church. Perhaps no critic of value-neutrality would want to go that far, but the question is not how far to go and where to stop (even if it were possible to stop at will—a supposition that is a clear 'fallacy of composition'). It is not one of the *degree* to which one may impose values and goals on others. It is, instead, a question of imposing, or not imposing, at all.

For strict liberalism, it cannot be *more* legitimate to impose values and goals that ought to inspire our choices, than to impose the choices themselves. If anything, it is less so, for a possible legitimising criterion may be satisfied by the latter but not by the former. If people, or groups of people, have strong feelings about certain issues, and find it important that others share these feelings, their sole legitimate resort is to persuasion and not to voting; coercion must be reserved for cases meeting far more demanding criteria. The potential for clash and contradiction between liberalism and democracy is discernible in this test case. For liberalism, it does not, but for democracy it does become mandatory for one person to submit to a decision because two or more others think very highly of the value it would serve.

Because questions of judgement, opinion, taste, relative valuation cannot be conclusively answered, it is a morally extraordinary pretension[1] to settle them by the power of collective

---

[1] The same pretension in a different guise used to be nurtured by the welfare economics of the inter-war and early post-war era. There was to be a conceivable social welfare function; maximising it was by definition better than failing to do so; therefore it was the proper function of society's collective instrument, the state, to maximise it. The shape and arguments of the supposed function were made known in the political process (voting, etc.) It took the influence of the much-derided logical positivists for welfare economics to withdraw from this far-out limb, and to concede that we cannot with any certainty say that some change of the *status quo* could be good unless it is at least a Pareto-improvement, and even if it is, we still cannot be sure that it is good.

choice, in favour of the protagonist having numbers (or, for that matter, anything else) on his side.

Coercion being illegitimate and a tort unless consented to, and because *proving consent is difficult*,[1] collective choice should clearly not be used to bring about a contested change on somebody's say-so that the change is good. Nothing in liberalism's rock-bottom principles authorises such *taking of sides*. Only when the change is uncontested, in the exacting sense of some welcoming and none rejecting it, can we hazard to say that it is very likely a change for the general good.

In all other cases, the strict liberal position is an agnostic one. It does not deny that some proposed collective option has merit; it does not claim to have the knowledge on which to base such a denial. It presumes, however, that if its merit were of the Pareto-superior kind that hurts no one's interest (and failing a plausible case that perverse incentives or socially redundant transactions costs prevent individuals choosing what they prefer), there would be some tendency towards it, some incipient move to choose it voluntarily, without coercion. If only coercion can resolve the issue, it is presumably wiser to be content to leave it unresolved.

Let it be added that an 'agnostic state' that has a general disposition to refrain from judging one value relative to others, and to diagnose the common good, the balance of advantage between advantages and drawbacks, gains and losses, need not condemn society to a paralytic, helpless acceptance of any *status quo* whatever. It is probably just as apt to induce it instead to develop talents and skills for finding conventional and contractual ways out. For it is hard to prove that a problem of society, if it is soluble at all, can be solved by collective choice but not by spontaneous co-operative arrangements, and there is no conceivable reason why the burden of proof should be on liberals and libertarians, and not on those who look to the state to solve it as a matter of course.

2. Choosing Constitutions

What I called above the 'parameters' of collective choice—*who* may choose for *whom*, and *what* may be chosen—must them-

---

[1] The absence of visible dissent is no proof of consent if expressing dissent is futile (and *a fortiori* when it is dangerous).

selves be chosen. This 'meta-choice' must be economical: lest we should have to bargain for a new one amongst ourselves in preparation for each and every collective choice, it must have the character of a stable rule, clear and generally understood, and 'sluggish' rather than 'agile' so as not to be prey to easy and frequent amendment. This is mainly why collective choice is usually governed by some formal or informal constitution, and why choosing a constitution is thought to be prior, and of a different moral and logical order, to the collective choices made according to its rules. For contractarians, the distinction between the choice of rules and choices within rules is a cardinal one, and the two are thought to be determined by two different sets of considerations—a view which I believe leads to illusory faith in the force of constitutions.

(a) Collective Choice, Chosen Individually

Collective choice being the non-violent means of reaching contested, non-unanimous decisions, it presupposes one of two possible motivations: *either* people submit peacefully to a particular collective choice to avoid being coerced to submit, *or* they do because they have consented in advance to accept whatever the decision will turn out to be, and are keeping their word. The former is the Humean, the latter the Hobbesian view, though we could tell which was the true view of submissive men's motives only if we could look into their heads. In the Hobbesian or socio-contractarian case, however, submission and promise-keeping have to be, and are, additionally secured by the coercion that is within the monopolistic power of collective choice ('Leviathan') to exert. Outwardly, therefore, the Humean and Hobbesian worlds are indistinguishable. Their justification, however, is different: socio-contractarian coercion is legitimate because consented to, and consent can be imputed to all who wish the promises of others to be enforceable.

It is of course outrageous to say that *A* consents to *B* being coerced. Therefore any theory that aspires to make coercion legitimate by imputing prior consent to the coercees, must make out some case that consent in the first place was unanimous. Failing initial unanimity, all might be coerced though only some have consented. Coercion would lose its justification in contract. Since unanimity is an aggregate of identical individual decisions, what needs to be shown is that the principle of collective choice, and its rules of operation, *would have been* individually chosen if rational persons had been confronted with these options. The latter, however, is equivalent to saying that collective choice, arrived at non-violently and free of bargaining costs—that is, simply by applying a pre-existing rule—is Pareto-superior to *no* rule. The legitimising primacy of individual choice and its non-dominated nature would thus be conferred upon collective choice as well.

In the basic kind of socio-contractarian thought that used to be current before it was challenged by public-choice theory, the assumption that at least some choices are intrinsically collective, and that avoiding violence in reaching them is universally preferred, sufficed to generate unanimous acceptance of some constitution in preference to none. Its specifications were left largely undefined except for the intimation that it must meet certain minimum *procedural* requirements. These relate to the subset designated to be decisive for making a choice binding on the whole set. By and large, the procedure must be 'democratic', depending on anonymous expressions of individual preference that shall be aggregated, and showing responsiveness to their sum. 'Democratically chosen' options are legitimately binding on all, and their enforcement is deemed to have been consented to in advance.

(b) Collective Choice, Chosen Collectively

The intrinsically dangerous, naked-razor nature of politics arises, not from politicians being cynical and bureaucrats incompetent, though it surely does not help if they are. The more basic and constant cause is that, like individual choice, collective choice, too, has a 'point' but, unlike it, realising the collective 'point' is not necessarily or even probably good for all concerned. The point of collective choice is precisely that, over most of the domain of its operation, it is bad for *some*.

Once its principle and its procedural rule are taken as consented to, collective choice acts as an instrument allowing the decisive subset of society to gain access to superior options (improve its material welfare, award itself rights), even if this means imposing inferior options on those outside the subset. In some plausible cases, the better the option it secures for itself, the worse will be the one imposed on the others. Redistributive options are of this kind. (They are often, somewhat loosely, called 'zero-sum', though it is not to be expected that the gain of the gainers should exactly offset the loss of the losers. The two may even be incommensurable.) However, at least within limits, a decisive subset is likely to be strongly motivated by its own gain and weakly, or not at all, deterred by the loss it inflicts on others.[1]

There is a wide field for speculation about possible secondary consequences. Maybe a so-called zero-sum exercise, if pushed far enough, turns into a negative-sum one, and maybe the negative sum grows large enough that even the winning subset ends up with an absolute loss. 'Excessive' redistribution would tautologically have to have this self-defeating effect.[2] Maybe the systematic exploitation of a wealthy or industrious minority will in the long run provoke it to withdraw its consent and upset the democratic applecart.

All this speculation, while not implausible, is inconclusive. Even if it could be credibly established that the choosers' gain from collective choice rises to some local maximum and falls beyond it, finally turning into a loss, it would still leave collective choice its leopard spots—either because it would actually be working towards its local maximum, or more probably because it would always suppose that there was still a way to go before reaching it.

Assume next that the unanimously chosen constitution did not stop at designating the subset entitled to choose for the set (a procedural rule), but went on to specify the kind of choice that was admissible (a substantive rule). For obvious reasons, it

---

[1] The envious are, of course, positively motivated by losses inflicted on others, by definition preferring to level downwards even without improving their own lot.

[2] Some economists hold that *any* redistribution must be 'excessive', that is, it must produce a negative sum for society by retarding the growth of wealth. In terms of the discounted present value of lifetime income, there will be, at plausible values of the relation between income inequality and saving, a net loss even to the apparent gainers. The latter may nevertheless persevere with the redistributive policy because of their 'weakness of will', mistrust of the *laissez-faire* argument in favour of inequality as a spur to growth, or simply because it is politically not feasible to kick the redistributive habit in exchange for a hypothetical gain in wealth that will not be noticeable before the next election.

might for example exclude from the domain of admissible choices anything that was unambiguously redistributive.[1] Exclusion of such choices could very well be assumed as a necessary condition of unanimous consent to the constitution, especially if the part of the community destined to find itself on the losing side of distributive justice-doing is credited with some foresight. (Apprehension of what might follow from simple majority rule over an unrestricted domain of legislative choice was implicitly on the mind of the framers of the American constitution, men of substance and above-average ability, most of whom could rightly expect to be exploited under such rules. Their precautions regarding the separation of powers, due process and the setting of obstacles to constitutional change, were ultimately of little avail.)

Suppose, in turn, that a substantive rule restricts the admissibility of certain choices (say, progressive taxation is barred and only proportional taxation is admitted), and a procedural rule strongly defends the substantive rule (say, a super-majority is needed to alter fundamental fiscal provisions). In the face of such belt-and-braces safeguards, the decisive subset can still pursue the same rational aim of maximising gains from collective choice by targeting, not the choices that are barred, but the rules that are barring them.

The constitution may well be 'sluggish', so that a larger decisive subset (e.g. a two-thirds majority) is needed to change it than to apply it. If this is the case, constitutional change can be obtained if there is a potential coalition of the required size; the incentive available for forming it is the potential gain released by a loosening of the restrictive constitution. The prospective losers

---

[1] By way of illustration, the Finnish constitution requires a five-sixth majority for laws overriding property rights. The taxation of income, however, does not pass for such, and does not need a super-majority. Consequently, the intended constitutional obstacle to redistribution is easily outflanked *via* routine fiscal policy on the income side of the state's budget, and by an inexhaustible assortment of possible policies on the expenditure side. Combinations of these policies can produce an inexhaustible variety of redistributive effects. This is not to suggest that Finnish governments have indulged in more transfers, subsidies, tax remissions, 'industrial policies', trade distortions, etc., than most others. It is merely to point out that declaring property rights inviolable (unless fully five-sixths of the legislature wanted to violate them) need not seriously hamper redistributive choices.

can never profitably overcompensate the potential members of the coalition, to persuade them not to coalesce. The bribe that would amount to an effective defence against a redistributive coalition is equal to the value that is being defended and that the coalition is out to get, making the defence pointless; for the losers either lose what they have, or spend it on the defence against its being taken from them.

The sequence of rational collective choices will then begin with transitory coalitions large or powerful enough to amend the rules or impose looser interpretations of them, thus getting closer to the maximising constitution, that is, one providing no obstacle to subsequent gain-maximising collective choices.

It is transparent that the maximising constitution must allow, *procedurally*, collective choice by the smallest possible subset, i.e. bare majority. This is a necessary property of the maximum because the larger is the losing subset whose interests can be overridden, the larger is the possible gain to the winning, decisive subset. Substantively, of course, any restriction of the domain of admissible choices is a potential constraint on maximisation of the gain. In order always to procure access to the dominant collective option, collective choice must be able to select alternatives according to how they are *ranked* by members of the winning subset and not according to what they *are*.[1]

This condition cannot generally be satisfied unless any option that is *available* is also constitutionally *admissible*. Relaxing the rules of admissibility is rewarded by the distribution of the gains that have been blocked by the rules, and that can be released by exploiting the losers whose interests the rules were protecting.

In sum, once non-violent politics is made possible by prior consent to non-unanimous decisions, the subset entitled to decide will be motivated to select, not only its best option admissible under a given constitutional rule, but also (and for the same reasons) the rule that admits the best options.[2] Collective

---

[1] The procedural (anonymity, bare majority rule) and the substantive (the substantive content of options does not influence their eligibility for collective choice; the people is sovereign) properties of the 'maximising constitution', taken together, appear to be equivalent to the ethical axioms that social choice theory postulates for acceptable choice rules ('social welfare functions').

[2] This theorem contradicts one strain of socio-contractarian theory, for which

[*Contd. on p. 118*]

choice, in other words, will be 'chosen collectively'. The dominant choice will be that under which no additional gains could be made by a further rule change. The constitutional choice rule will be in final equilibrium when it can no longer be made any more 'democratic'.

3. Legitimacy, Procedural and Substantive

(a) Redistributive Choices

Consenting to politics, by agreeing in advance to abide by non-unanimous choices reached under a chosen rule, thus proves to be something of a trap. Its catch is that each rule is associated with gains the winners under the particular rule can make at the expense of the losers. By striking bargains over the sharing out of the potential gains, it is always possible to find a coalition that could profit from replacing a rule that severely limits redistribution by one that limits it only a little, or not at all.

There is, however, no morally defensible reason for accepting the coercion involved in collective choice if the latter is able to write its own rules. Its justification in that case becomes perfectly circular: *collective choice chooses itself.* Can it, then, be consistent with strict liberal doctrine, that must legitimise coercion by imputing individual consent to it, to advise people to step into the trap?—and can it possibly be prevented from snapping shut?

We could learn it from experience, if we could not infer it from the very nature of the problem, that historically collective choice has a tendency, more or less pronounced depending on the tides of politics, wars and trade, to encroach upon individual choice. The growing relative rôle of government provides qualitative, and the long-term trend of public expenditure as a proportion of national income quantitative evidence of its constancy. Knowing this and yet to concede that collective choice is admissible under strict liberalism, is knowingly to accept rigged odds against its possible survival as a political order. In winding up the present work, I propose briefly to consider the argument

---

choices 'within rules' are made according to one set of behavioural assumptions or motives (*cf.* 'public choice'), while the choice of rules is made according to another (*cf.* 'the veil of uncertainty' or 'ignorance'). The contradiction is partly a matter of empirical fact, partly of questionable logical inference from the common assumptions of rationality.

in favour of politics that strict liberalism is bound to reject, and the one it may have to accept. The former relates to re-distribution, the latter to public goods.

It must squarely be faced that redistributive choices contradict the non-domination principle, and that liberalism as a *distinct* political doctrine, that we can tell apart from others, stands or falls with that principle. The losers under such choices would prefer not to lose; the substantive outcome is Pareto-inferior and is not value-neutral. An agnostic government has no conceivable basis for adjudicating in its favour. Nor is coercion or its threat to give effect to the redistributive choice legitimate. Strict liberalism makes in this respect a sharp departure from standard social contract doctrine under which coercion to enforce a collective choice is legitimate if, and because, the procedure employed in reaching it is a legitimate procedure. For the strict liberal, a collective choice made constitutionally (in the sense of con-formity to a rule that could reasonably have been agreed by all) may still be an unwarranted use of the power of collective choice. This is so principally because rules can conceivably be unani-mously agreed without being purged of circular, *self-referring* properties which enable strict rules to be non-unanimously relaxed, permitting collective choice to choose its own scope.

(b) Prisoners, or Hawk-and-Dove

Next to redistributive ones, the other class of intrinsically collective choices uses coercion or its latent threat to enforce co-operative arrangements, principally conventions and contracts, whose particular characteristics would defeat self-enforcement.

The really problematic enforcement-dependent arrangement is the *contract* of *non-simultaneous exchange*, where one party (a person or a group) has a clear incentive to default once the other party has performed as promised. In conventions with an analogous structure of incentives, deviation from the con-ventional norm becomes the best option once enough others have conformed to it.

If the second performer in a contract can do best for himself by defaulting, it seems foolhardy for the first performer to perform. The upshot is that failing enforcement, so to speak from the outside, there can be no credible contract with non-simultaneous performances. There will then be great difficulty in securing reliable mutual commitments to schemes of co-operation that would benefit all parties; the parties are in a 'prisoners' dilemma'.[1] Plainly, if the coercive force of collective choice can deter default and render such a contract credible, far from imposing on the parties a dominated option, it will help them take the dominant one. Consequently, collective choice is applied to a situation, as it were remedially. The attendant coercion, like medicine, would be agreed to by rational individuals, and is legitimate. Its legitimacy is not merely procedural—the choice is made in an agreed manner—but substantive—the choice leads to an outcome (at least weakly) preferred by all concerned.

The classic co-operative arrangement that is held to require collectively imposed contract enforcement is the production of public goods, being any tangible or intangible good to which individuals have access[2] independently of any contribution they may or may not have made to producing it. For a public good, there is no relation between an individual's marginal benefit and his marginal cost. When a good is provided publicly, a taxpayer

---

[1] In game-theory language, the dominant strategy of each player is one that secures for him the highest pay-off regardless of what strategy the other player adopts. Each could expect a better pay-off by co-operating provided the other did, too. But *if* the other co-operated, the first player could have secured an *even better* pay-off by not co-operating. The best thus becomes an enemy of the better. Each player will have non-co-operation as his dominant strategy that yielded a better pay-off than co-operation both when the other player chose to co-operate and when he did not.

A crucial condition for this sub-optimal equilibrium is that the players move instantaneously, hence being unable to make their moves tentative and contingent on the move of the other player. In the latter case, their strategy could be: 'I start co-operating when you do, and stop if and when you stop'. This strategy could permit a Pareto-optimal equilibrium solution.

[2] Most textbook definitions of public goods imply *unlimited* access: everyone can consume as much as he wishes without anybody having to consume any less as a result. However, this is really a limiting case. In the general case, an increased benefit to one consumer may result in a reduced one to another; the good may be 'crowded' to varying extents. Such is the case of a road, bridge or other public facility that has a fixed capacity (as more traffic uses the road, it is less convenient for each to use it).

The essential condition of publicness is not 'non-rivalry in consumption', but the lack of a direct nexus between benefit and contribution (that is, costless access to the good at the margin), which in turn is a consequence of 'non-exclusion': all have access to some benefit whether or not they pay.

can use it more or less, without paying more or less tax as a consequence. Voluntary contribution to such a good is irrational if one can have access to it anyway. Since this is true for all, no one would contribute voluntarily, hence a public good could never be produced, though all would like to have it. Overcoming the dilemma is thought to require a contract, collectively enforced, under which all contribute because they must, and none is too unhappy since he can safely count on all others doing so. Agreement to be taxed is the logical equivalent of such a contract: hence it is potentially unanimous and being held to it by coercion is substantively legitimate.

This line of argument which (complete with complicated arrangements of bells and whistles) underlies the explanation and normative defence of the state by modern welfare economics, is less compelling and general than it looks. It is contingent on the facts of the case. It is not generally true that the incentive structure of a co-operative enterprise, for instance to produce public goods, would necessarily favour non-co-operation.[1] If it does not, voluntary co-operation may not be uniform—some may be more 'civic' than others—but a sufficient proportion of a good's prospective consumers may find it worth while to help produce it for a whole community. Their commitment to do so can be self-enforcing, or if it is insufficiently so, it may be enforced under a satellite arrangement (*cf.* the enforcement of queueing, see Ch.5), the two together being 'ultimately self-enforcing'.

All that the economics of rational choice can tell us about the necessity and efficiency of choosing collectively, is that public goods will or will not be produced by the voluntary co-operation of some interested parties (the 'doves' among the 'hawks'),

---

[1] Using game-theory language again, the pay-offs associated with alternative strategies need not form a 'prisoners' dilemma'. They may, under plausible assumptions, form a game of 'hawk-and-dove' instead, where *no strategy is best*, and it may be as rational for some to contribute (play 'dove') as for others to default (play 'hawk').

Moreover, still under plausible assumptions, for all players taken together a 'mixed strategy' is better than either pure hawkishness or pure doveishness. An individual who expects too many others to play 'hawk' will then choose to play 'dove', or *vice versa*. Thus the group as a whole will tend to conform to the mixed strategy, some of its members contributing to a co-operative endeavour, others 'riding free'.

depending on the cost of exclusion, the cost of private substitutes, and the probability each party attaches to others being 'doves' or 'hawks'—that is, willing or refusing to co-operate.

It is possible, and under plausible parameters indeed likely, that at least some public goods, such as observance and administration of the common law, including the protection of life and property and the enforcement of contracts where necessary, as well as infrastructural facilities, would be provided. These goods would be forthcoming, albeit in a patchy, unsystematic, particularist manner by schemes of *ad hoc*, spontaneous, often locally confined co-operation *if* there were no systematic, uniform, nation-wide compulsory arrangements for them. It is morally certain that under compulsory arrangements more, perhaps far more, public goods are produced. But it does not follow from any obvious principle, nor from any observed fact, that these are produced because they are 'necessary', nor that their volume is 'efficient'. If anything can support the argument for taxation to produce public goods, it is a severe case-by-case, good-by-good scrutiny, and then only tentatively, uncertainly and subject to continual re-assessment.

Hence the political choice is not, as we have been conditioned to believe for generations, a sweeping one: it is not either order or chaos, either public goods with coercion or spontaneity but no public goods. Rather is it a range of alternatives, with a borderline extreme of *certainty* of a wide (and expanding) variety of public goods, chosen collectively and contributed to compulsorily. Moving away from certainty, the alternatives extend over the entire scale of probabilities that various items in a narrower selection of public goods will be supplied under imperfect, incomplete case-by-case civic arrangements.

The ideal test of 'substantively legitimate' coercion, then, would be evidence that non-coerced, voluntary attempts at providing some public good have been and are being made, but fail. If no attempt has been made, the case for providing it by collective choice is suspect. Those who say they need it seek to get it on free-rider terms. Their willingness to contribute its marginal cost remains untested.

It goes without saying that no voluntary attempt makes practical sense if the state provides the good anyway. Consequently, the test of voluntariness has little or no scope where the state is a fully-fledged going concern and collective choices are profusely and routinely made. The test then is merely a thought-experiment, a prescription for critical scrutiny, for case-by-case inquiry, where the burden of proof is on those who argue, both that a public good is a dominant option people would rather be taxed for than go without, and that it can best be chosen collectively.

4. Limited Government

My purpose has been to find and put forward minimal principles that could serve as the rock-bottom foundation for a strict and stable version of liberalism, and to develop their implications. The intended result was the elementary outline of an abstract political doctrine. Two ready-made counts are promptly at hand for dismissing it: that it is abstract, and that it is a doctrine. Perhaps it is not surprising if, having argued for it, I plead that the temptation to dismiss it too quickly should be resisted.

The purpose of a doctrine is to serve as a rough-and-ready guide, a rudimentary compass telling us where we are headed, on or off course for where we want to arrive. Lacking a doctrine, every question stands on its own, independent of every other. There is no ready way of telling whether the answers we give to each are mutually compatible, and no economies can be found to reduce the information costs of being governed, nor of governing the government. The more abstract the doctrine, the more general and wide-angled is the perspective that shows alternative policies and their likely consequences in relation to one another.

Instead of setting up the standard liberal objectives of freedom and limited government, and designing a political order maximising the chances of their attainment—an approach which, like other value- and goal-oriented designs, is as likely to frustrate these objectives as to foster them—and instead of assuming the existence of certain rights that presuppose that all must accept the corresponding obligations, I have advanced along a line that I believe presupposes less than either of these types of design. Proceeding from relatively undemanding first principles can, it would seem, establish some disposition toward freedom and limited government without explicitly calling for them. I say 'disposition' advisedly, for the most one can hope for in this respect is to improve the odds.

Holding collective decisions to the rules of procedural legitimacy born of consent is secondary to the issue. Democratically reached decisions are no less apt to result in domination over individual options and an expansion of the power of collective choice, than the 'arbitrary will' of dictatorship. Designing the right sort of constitution would render democratic power harmless, benign if constitutional design were really decisive for the way collective choice operated. But since law can change law, judges make law, politics makes judges and interest and opinion make politics, in the last analysis collective choice can always write its own rules. It should cause no surprise that its built-in propensity is to shape and interpret the rules of a constitution so as to maximise its own capacity to serve the purposes of winners in contested choices—a propensity that lends procedural legitimacy to expanding government.

Limited government is one that *both* observes procedural legitimacy *and* stays within substantive legitimacy. Since much that is procedurally legitimate may go well beyond what is substantively so, respect for procedure does not even probabilistically help substantive legitimacy. If anything does, it is people's own taboos about the use of the power of collective choice, their sense of what is proper and fitting, their readiness or reluctance to award themselves rights, and their ideas and prejudices about how a social system can be made to function. These are, at the end of the day, metaphysical commitments. They determine preferences and interests at least as much as, if not more so than, being determined by them. In this lies their potential for keeping collective choice from using all the irresistible power that is within its grasp. Political doctrines shape the political order, not by dictating its design, but essentially by inducing people to make certain metaphysical commitments. Restating liberalism in a strict and, I trust, reasonably coherent version is meant to contribute to the 'right' commitments.